HALLOWEEN
TOWN

Disney

Tim Burton's The Nightmare Before Christmas

THE ULTIMATE VISUAL HISTORY

THE ULTIMATE VISUAL HISTORY

By Dana Jennings Jelter

INSIGHT
EDITIONS

SAN RAFAEL • LOS ANGELES • LONDON

CONTENTS

FOREWORD

"T'was a long time ago, longer now than it seems . . . "

Rick Heinrichs wouldn't explain why he needed to fly up and meet with me. Rick had sculpted Jack, Zero, and Santa Claus for Tim's first pitch of *The Nightmare Before Christmas* to Disney in 1982. Originally, Tim had envisioned a holiday stop-motion special, one that would air every year on TV, but Disney couldn't see it. Rick told me that he and Tim admired my stop-motion work for MTV, including the *Slow Bob* in the *Lower Dimensions* pilot I'd just completed. Then the bombshell came: It was 1990, and Disney had agreed to make *Nightmare* as a stop-motion feature—and Tim wanted me to direct it!

It's hard to believe it's been over thirty years since we made *Tim Burton's The Nightmare Before Christmas*. Before we even had a finished script, *Nightmare* began production with just a few songs and a general sense of the story. Michael McDowell, who'd written *Beetlejuice* (1988), took a stab at the script, but his health was poor, and his contributions were limited. I'm pretty sure he gave us the haunting moment where Sally jumps from the tower, shatters, and then stitches herself back together.

Stop-motion animation is an unforgiving art form. There's no room for mistakes. You lock in the camera moves and lighting, rehearse, and then take the leap—frame by frame. You improvise and adjust as you go, willing the character to life. The team on *Nightmare* was made up of passionate, skilled artists who put their souls into every shot.

We made the film in San Francisco, at a warehouse that had been converted into a shooting stage. The handprints of Whoopi Goldberg, Rip Torn, and Hervé Villechaize were embedded in the concrete. Just as we began to shoot, construction started on a new jail next door, with pile drivers shaking our sets and puppets every ten seconds, all day long. Not ideal for stop-motion animation.

The film was low-tech in every sense—shot on film, with effects like ghosts, fire, and sparks all shot in-camera. If a puppet fell mid-shot, the whole scene was ruined. Later, we discovered a digital frame grabber. It could only capture two frames (one-twelfth of a second), but now, if a puppet broke, the team would fix it and line up its pose with the frames we had already shot.

One of the challenges we faced was staying true to Tim's unique vision. This was difficult because Tim's style is so specific. Art director Deane Taylor was already close to it, and assistant art directors Kelly Asbury and Kendall Cronkhite soon learned to channel Tim in their own designs. Bo Henry, head set builder, came up with the idea of 2D/3D sets that looked like the etchings Tim loved, raking wet plaster on plywood to give *Nightmare* its distinctive look. There was a lot of trial and error, which all paid off in the end.

Tim, Danny Elfman, and I all shared Jack Skellington. Tim dreamed him up and designed him, Danny wrote his songs and gave him his singing voice, and I embodied Jack's physicality, acting him out for the animators. In a way, all three of us became Jack in the process.

When screenwriter Caroline Thompson came on board, she beautifully stitched together Danny's songs with the story and added depth and soul to Sally and her relationship with Jack. Caroline's Sally is much like my wife, Heather, who admires my Jack-like passion for projects but also cares for me despite my many flaws. Those feelings seeped into my direction of both Sally and Jack in the film.

Our crew was small but incredibly talented—including Joe Ranft, Head of Story, genius DP Pete Kozachik, who hand-built our huge motion control rigs, producer Kathleen Gavin, Animation Lead Animator Eric Leighton, and many more. Everyone knew everyone else's name and worked relentlessly with grace and good humor. Our 14 animators—Paul Berry, Tim Hittle, Angie Glocka, Anthony Scott, and Mike Belzer, among others—were all world-class. One of our best, Trey Thomas, wiped out on his motorcycle one night at a railroad crossing. I rushed over and asked how he was. "Just a little road rash," he replied. The next day, he animated some of the finest Sally movements in the whole film.

Under Bonita DeCarlo's supervision, all our puppets were built by hand, from the metal armatures that could bend and twist, to the bodies sculpted around them, to the final costumes, hair, and paint. It took real craftsmanship. Tim

wanted Jack to be tall and thin—challenging, since stop-motion puppets need sturdy armatures to support their weight. So, Jack's shoes were made of painted metal. Sally was more voluptuous, so her stronger ankles were hidden under her striped socks. This attention to detail helped bring the characters to life in a way that felt completely real.

Finding Santa's voice proved to be a challenge. Vincent Price, Tim's idol, was too heartbroken after losing his wife. James Earl Jones, the voice of Darth Vader, was too thunderous. Eventually, we found the perfect Santa in local San Francisco actor Ed Ivory, who had the warmth and presence we needed.

Danny Elfman's eleven songs are the heart of the film. Initially, I worried we might lose the audience around song six or seven. And when we finished the film, Tim agreed and suggested we cut one or two. I said absolutely not, and the murder in my eyes changed his mind. In time, every song became an integral part of the film's success. It's strange and wonderful how *Nightmare* grew into something that captured the imagination of so many people. The animation, the lighting, the characters, the songs, the story—all of it just clicked.

It wasn't all intense work and late nights—there was crazy fun, too. Leaving one night, I discovered my entire car had been covered in sticky notes. Raucous hooting began in the rafters. I looked up to find the culprits—artists Bill Boes and Mike Cachuela—acting like deranged chimps. Then there was that Halloween party, where producer Kathleen Gavin showed up as animator Paul Berry, her costume perfectly capturing the Brit's fashion sense and flaming red hair.

In many ways, *Nightmare* was a fluke. We had no digital technology, no huge budget, no big-name stars—just a core group of talented people who loved the material and were determined to make something special. And somehow, we did. It wasn't an easy road, but in the end, *The Nightmare Before Christmas* found its audience, and it continues to capture the imagination of fans around the world. I look back on it with immense pride—what we made was something unique and truly special. And I hope that, as you read through these pages, you get a sense of how that magic came to life, frame by frame, song by song, idea by idea.

Thank you for being part of *Nightmare*'s journey.

—HENRY SELICK

PAGE 2: Theatrical poster for *Tim Burton's The Nightmare Before Christmas*.

PAGE 5: Concept art of Halloween Town by art director Deane Taylor.

THIS PAGE: Henry Selick, director of *Tim Burton's The Nightmare Before Christmas*.

INTRODUCTION

Before *Tim Burton's The Nightmare Before Christmas* ever flickered to life on screen, it was a shadowy idea conjured from the mind of Tim Burton—a love letter to all things strange and spooky. First imagined as a poem in the early 1980s and brought to life a decade later through the magic of stop-motion animation, the film has since become a genre-defying classic that endures across generations. What began as an unconventional holiday story grew into a cultural phenomenon: a Halloween-Christmas hybrid film that carved out its own permanent place in pop culture.

This book is your backstage pass to the making of that phenomenon. Within these pages, you'll find rare behind-the-scenes photographs, original concept art, and exclusive interviews with the creative team that brought Halloween Town and its cast of misfit characters to life. From early sketches of Jack Skellington to the meticulous process of animating dozens of incredible puppets, this visual guide peels back the curtain on a production that was as imaginative and intricate as the film itself.

In many ways, *Tim Burton's The Nightmare Before Christmas* was a gamble. At a time when computer-generated imagery was beginning to dominate animation, the idea of crafting an entire feature-length film using stop-motion puppets and hand-built sets seemed almost anachronistic—a lingering relic of cinema's past. But that only made

PAGES 8–9: Concept art of the Hinterlands, drawn by assistant art director Kendal Cronkhite.

TOP: Author Dana Jennings Jelter in Japan.

PAGES 12–13: Concept art of the snow-covered Christmas Town village by assistant art director Kendal Cronkhite.

it more appealing to a ragtag group of off-kilter artists, led by a self-proclaimed outsider in Burton himself. The stop-motion process is slow and precise—twenty-four individual frames for every second of film—but it's this level of craft that gives the movie its distinct texture. You can almost feel it under your fingertips.

Director Henry Selick, working closely with Burton and producer Denise Di Novi, leaned into the tactile charm and surreal elegance of stop-motion, creating a world that felt hand-carved and hauntingly alive. Every frame—literally—was sculpted with care, animated by hand, and lit like a dream (or a nightmare) to achieve a level of mood and detail few films had attempted before or since.

What also makes the film so enduring is its emotional resonance. Jack Skellington may be the Pumpkin King, but his dissatisfaction with routine and yearning for something new is deeply human. When he stumbles into Christmas Town and attempts to reinvent himself—and the holiday—he sets off a chain of events both comedic and poignant. This duality runs throughout the film: light and dark, joy and melancholy, control and chaos. It's a fairy tale for the weird at heart, one that embraces the misunderstood and finds beauty in the bizarre.

In telling the story behind this magical film, we'll explore the many creative minds who contributed to this vision. You'll meet the animators, artists, and technicians who worked tirelessly over several years to construct this collaborative work of art. Their innovations in puppet mechanics, practical effects, and lighting pushed the boundaries of what stop-motion could do—and influenced an entire generation of animators and filmmakers.

You'll also read about the role of music in shaping the narrative. Composer Danny Elfman didn't just write songs for the film—he sang them, embodying Jack Skellington's longing and excitement in a way that remains iconic. The songs are stitched together into a tapestry of varied genres: part Broadway musical, part carnival melody, part twisted lullaby. Elfman's score is a central character in its own right, guiding the emotional rhythm of the story and helping define the film's unique tone.

And then there's the film's legacy. What began as a niche favorite upon its 1993 release grew into a holiday classic, then a merchandising empire, and finally a beloved staple of both Halloween and Christmas traditions. Fans now cosplay as every character, collect the most obscure memorabilia, and sing every lyric at live concert screenings. Disney transforms entire sections of their theme parks to resemble Halloween Town each year. The film's aesthetic has become a language of its own—instantly recognizable, eerily charming, and eternally cool.

Yet despite its popularity, *Tim Burton's The Nightmare Before Christmas* has always remained a bit of an outsider, much like its protagonist. It exists beyond categorization, floating between holidays, genres, and age groups. Is it a kids' film? A gothic romance? A musical comedy? A horror story? The answer is yes, it's all these things and more, stitched together like one of Dr. Finkelstein's creepy yet endearing creations.

As you journey through this book, rediscover the magic and madness that went into making *Tim Burton's The Nightmare Before Christmas*. Whether you're a longtime fan or taking your first trip to Halloween Town, may this visual guide deepen your appreciation for a film that proved a world built by hand—crooked, careful, and completely original—can speak louder than anything polished or perfect.

—DANA JENNINGS JELTER

Cafe

CHAPTER 1

“’TWAS A LONG TIME AGO . . .”: *NIGHTMARE*’S ANIMATED BEGINNINGS

“It’s a long process, and it’s not everybody’s cup of tea . . . It’s how I lost my hair.”
—RAY HARRYHAUSEN, *JASON AND THE ARGONAUTS* (1963)

On October 22, 1993, Roger Ebert wrote a review for *Tim Burton’s The Nightmare Before Christmas*. In his review, he suggested readers see the film more than once. “First, go for the story. Then go back just to look in the corners of the screen and appreciate the little visual surprises and inspirations that are tucked into every nook and cranny.”

Many of those special visual surprises and little details are a by-product of a world created entirely from scratch. Each building, prop, fabric, and even strand of hair was created by human hands that sparked life into the creepy, imaginary world we all know and love. Stop-motion films often gain a following. They may have small numbers at the box office upon their initial release, but they gain high popularity over time through merchandise sales, streaming numbers, and rereleases. The intricacies and effort required by the stop-motion process; the fantastical realism of the puppets, props, and sets; and the unique stories often told with this style of animation are key ingredients that cultivate a dedicated fan base. To create this special connection with the audience, animators must make people think they can reach out and grab a character by the hand—and in the world of stop-motion, that’s a reality.

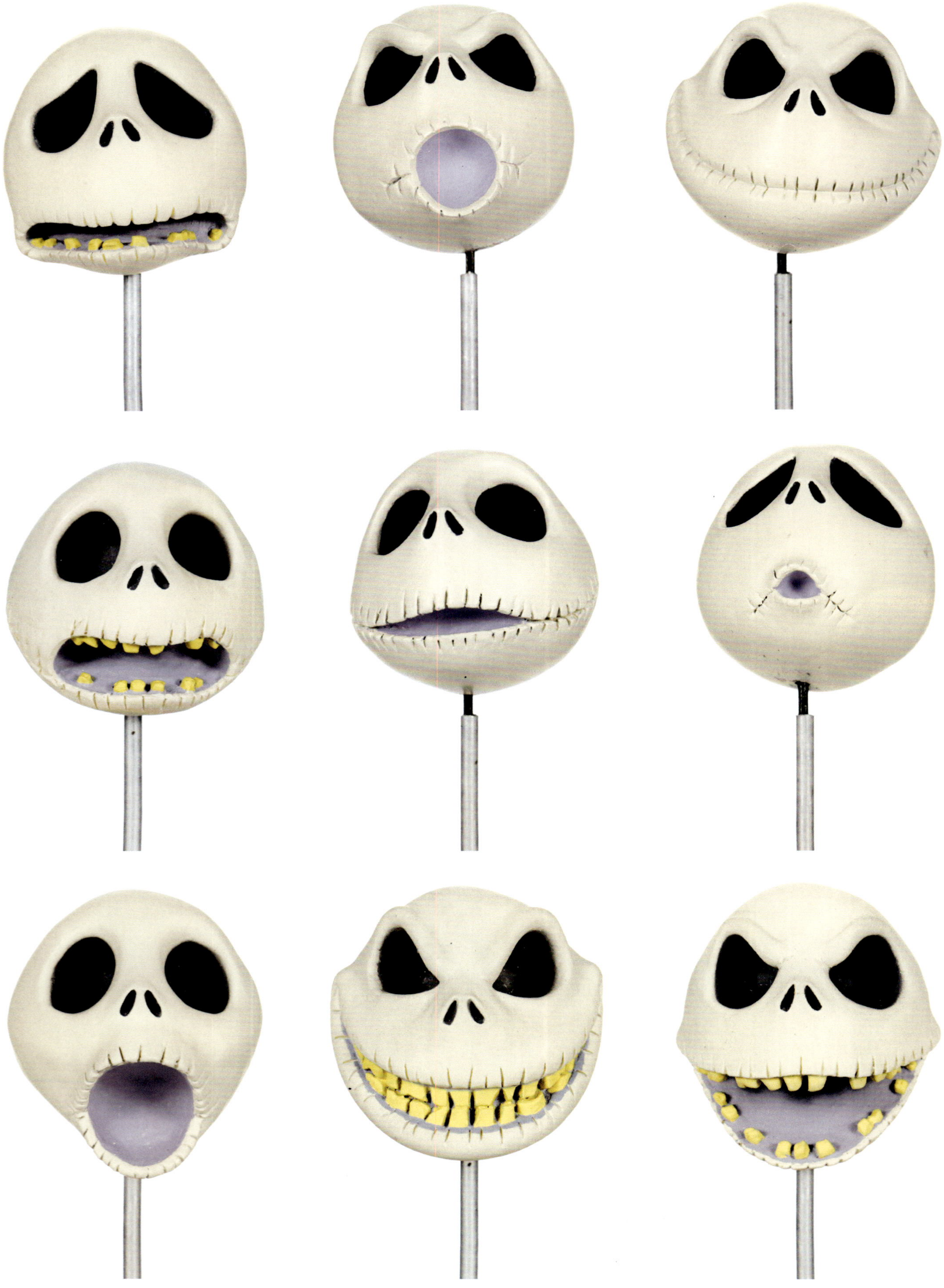

STARTING WITH STOP TRICK

Many consider *Tim Burton's The Nightmare Before Christmas* to be a groundbreaking animated feature, but the technical inspiration behind its genius dates back well over a century. The origins of stop-motion animation are often debated, though it's commonly believed to have started with a mistake. Around 1895, filmmaker Georges Méliès was filming a busy street in Paris when his camera jammed. He opened his camera, fixed the film, and resumed filming, only to find that when he watched the clip later, his scene had seemingly transformed. Men were replaced by women and a bus changed into a hearse. This inspired Méliès to use this accidental technique as a form of trickery, and it wasn't long until "stop trick" was being used in the United States, ushering in waves of stop-motion animators throughout the twentieth century.

Also in 1895, Thomas Edison's production company released *The Execution of Mary Stuart*, a jaw-dropping film for the time. In only eighteen seconds, director Alfred Clark appeared to capture an actual beheading—though, in reality, he simply paused filming, replaced a live actor with a mannequin, and resumed filming again. Audiences in the late 1890s, who were mostly unfamiliar with how motion pictures worked, could not fathom how he was able to capture something like this on film. Many believed the actress in the film actually gave her life for the success of the motion picture. It was certainly disturbing, and along with other creepy "stop-trick" films like J. Stuart Blackton's *The Haunted Hotel* (1907) and Émile Cohl's *Bewitched Matches* (1913), the genre was often tied to more frightening features. The rudimentary puppets brought to life through jerky movements brewed a feeling of unease that was perfect for scary storytelling.

The Humpty Dumpty Circus (1898), a film created by J. Stuart Blackton and Albert E. Smith, is thought to be the first American film to actually use stop-motion to animate, rather than just displace objects. It was also the first film in which animation was created through moving posable toys rather than household objects or real people. Smith used his daughter's wooden circus toy set, and with the animals' movable joints, he was able to reposition them each time he exposed a new frame.

In the 1910s, stop-motion saw the unique style of Polish-Russian historian-turned-animator Wladyslaw Starewicz. While working in a natural history museum, Starewicz wished to film a fight between two stag beetles, but he couldn't get them to perform under the bright lights required for filming. To remedy this, he began to use dead, dried beetles articulated with wire and wax and posed and animated them via stop-motion. Many credit Starewicz's *The Cameraman's Revenge* (1912), about a love triangle involving a beetle, a dragonfly, and a grasshopper, as the first animated film to use "puppets." Seven decades later, visual consultant Rick Heinrichs would show Starewicz's film, and his grotesque method of animating the actual dead, to his colleagues while they animated the fictional undead in *Tim Burton's The Nightmare Before Christmas*.

PAGE 14: Jack Skellington sings in front of the neon-green sludge that is the water source of Halloween Town.

OPPOSITE: Replacement heads for Jack Skellington.

RIGHT: Jack lands in Christmas Town.

ANCIENT TALES AND CREATURES

The 1920s and 1930s were, of course, dominated by hand-drawn, 2D animation produced by the likes of Max Fleischer (*Betty Boop*), Walt Disney, and Ub Iwerks (legendary early Disney animator). However, stop-motion continued to gain popularity for animators who valued the tangible quality of the art. As *Tim Burton's The Nightmare Before Christmas* director Henry Selick describes it, stop-motion "has a primal nature. It can never be perfect." This alluring imperfection kept the art alive alongside new forms of animation throughout the twentieth century.

In 1926, *The Adventures of Prince Achmed*, an animated film by Lotte Reiniger, utilized the technique of silhouette (or cutout) animation with cardboard and lead sheets. Selick has named that film as one of his biggest inspirations for becoming an animator, and it currently holds the title of oldest surviving animated feature film. In *Nightmare*, this same silhouette aesthetic was borrowed in the scenes of Oogie Boogie's shadow on the moon and during the character's first reveal in his lair.

Around the same time Reiniger was bringing old Middle Eastern folktales to life, Willis O'Brien was beginning to resurrect dinosaurs. O'Brien, known commonly as Obie, worked as a nature guide for University of Southern California scientists in Crater Lake, Oregon, sparking his passion for archeology and prehistoric creatures. That fascination, paired with a later sculpting job in a San Francisco marble shop, set him on his path to creating and animating the most realistic dinosaur models at the time.

O'Brien's most famous films, *The Lost World* (1925) and *King Kong* (1933), evoked a sensation of awe and wonder reminiscent of Clark's footage for Edison of Mary Stuart's beheading in 1895. His dinosaur puppets made people question reality. Surely, dinosaurs are extinct, so how did O'Brien bring them to life so clearly? One puzzled young viewer was Ray Harryhausen, probably the most notable stop-motion animator in American cinema.

Harryhausen's animation career began in 1940 with a job working for another stop-motion giant, George Pal. Pal's "Puppetoons" were animated films featuring childlike wooden puppets—the first to utilize the replacement technique in stop-motion. Rather than changing the position of the puppet or reshaping clay, Pal replaced heads, body parts, or entire puppets for each frame to change expressions or simulate movement. This technique greatly improved the efficiency of puppet animation, and it's still used in stop-motion features today: The Jack puppets (there were many duplicates) of *Tim Burton's The Nightmare Before Christmas* included a collection of almost 400 interchangeable heads to convey his colorful emotions. (See page 104, "The Head Replacement Technique.")

Harryhausen eventually went on to work with Willis O'Brien as an assistant animator on *Mighty Joe Young* (1949). Though the film didn't achieve the success of its predecessor *King Kong*, it took home a 1950 Academy Award for Best Visual Effects, which was certainly a milestone for a film featuring stop-motion. More than forty years later, *Nightmare* was also nominated for a Best Visual Effects Oscar—making it the first fully animated film to be nominated in this category.

OPPOSITE: Sketch of Jack Skellington's home by art director Deane Taylor and assistant art director Kendal Cronkhite.

FROM GUMBY TO GROMIT

The 1950s and 1960s saw the success of Art Clokey's *The Gumby Show*. Gumby, the friendly, green glob of clay, is essentially the first stop-motion icon. Though his design was simple, his stories had heart, and children were drawn to the playful animation style. His likeness was featured on toys and merchandise, including coloring books, magnets, and even jewelry. He paved the way for the characters of *Tim Burton's The Nightmare Before Christmas*, which later covered lunch boxes and beach towels—among thousands of other items. Gumby influenced *Nightmare* in another way: Many of the animators who worked on Tim Burton's iconic film got their start working on Clokey Productions.

Talk to any animator—from Tim Burton and Henry Selick to British animators like Sam Fell (codirector of LAIKA's *ParaNorman*, 2012) and Peter Lord (cofounder of Aardman Animations)—and many, if not all, will claim that Ray Harryhausen inspired their career in one way or another. His invention of the technique he coined "dynamation" combined live action with stop-motion. The result was a puzzling but nearly seamless depiction of humans and creatures inhabiting the same space. Selick recalls a fascination with the cyclops in Harryhausen's *The 7th Voyage of Sinbad* (1958), the first movie he saw in a theater with his scary movie-loving mom at the age of five.

OPPOSITE: The cyclops from Ray Harryhausen's *The 7th Voyage of Sinbad* (1958).

BOTTOM: The stop-motion skeletons seen in *Jason and the Argonauts* (1963), featuring Todd Armstrong as Jason.

STOP-MO TERMS TO KNOW

DYNAMATION: A form of animation created by legendary stop-motion animator Ray Harryhausen that allows real actors to interact with stop-motion characters.

The film clearly inspired Selick's love of creepy creatures, and the cyclops even made his way into *Nightmare*'s cast of characters in Halloween Town. "I remember I had a recurring nightmare about the cyclops being small and growing ever larger in this big fish tank we had at our house," he says. "The dream was it was getting bigger and bigger and was going to break out and come and get me. But over time, I started looking forward to meeting it."

When it comes to naming stop-motion legends, or just animation pioneers in general, Harryhausen is truly at the top of the list. His film *Jason and the Argonauts* (1963) is one of his most notable works, mainly due to the jaw-dropping skeleton battle. The scene features seven stop-motion skeletons fighting three live actors, and it took more than four months to produce the four-minute scene.

Tim Burton first saw *Jason and the Argonauts* as a child in the 1960s at the Avalon Theatre on Catalina Island. The Avalon's art deco interior design meshed with Harryhausen's masterpiece, and the memory had a lasting effect. Burton recalls, "I remember both the theater and the movie because they seemed to be as one, the design of the theater, that movie, and the kind of mythology it evoked. It was incredible."

The filmmaker describes *Jason and the Argonauts* as "strong, and goes right inside you and sticks with you like a dream." As for Harryhausen, "[He] was always a singular artist. It was like he was an actor; he was like the character. There was a personal feeling about the medium and the way he sort of infused it that made it a strong, visceral experience. The way all the monsters died, there was just a real sense of emotion in there that was really interesting."

TOP: Young Rudolph as seen in the television special *Rudolph the Red-Nosed Reindeer* (1964), from Rankin/Bass Productions.

ABOVE: A sketch of Jack as the Pumpkin King.

ABOVE RIGHT: A sketch of Jack playing as Santa Claus.

FARTHER RIGHT: Concept art of Jack Skellington by assistant art director Kelly Asbury.

INFLUENCES FROM HOME AND ABROAD

The stop-motion animation specials from the 1960s were a big inspiration to Tim Burton. He, like many children in the sixties, was introduced to the animation style through the film specials of Arthur Rankin Jr. and Jules Bass, known collectively through their production company, Rankin/Bass. Though they started out strictly in advertising, they collaborated with Japanese animator Tadahito Mochinaga from 1960 to 1967 to bring their film creations to life using the stop-motion technique they called "animagic." The most popular Rankin/Bass holiday specials are *Rudolph the Red-Nosed Reindeer* (1964) and *Santa Claus is Comin' to Town* (1970), though Tim Burton's personal favorite was *Mad Monster Party?* (1967). "People thought *Nightmare* was the first stop-motion animated monster musical," he says, "but that was."

Along with the influences of Harryhausen and Rankin/Bass, *Nightmare*'s unique style was also influenced by European stop-motion. Burton recalls seeing a documentary as a child about Czech animator Karel Zeman and his film *The Fabulous Baron Munchausen* (1962). The way Zeman emphasized the handmade quality of his films inspired Burton to do the same with his own art.

Henry Selick has referenced Jan Švankmajer as one of the few stop-motion animators to influence *Nightmare*'s style. The Czech surrealist created a number of short films in the 1960s and 1970s that combined stop-motion and live action to create an offbeat, nightmarish vibe. Švankmajer's 1971 short film *Jabberwocky*, based loosely on the poem by Lewis Carroll, seems to be a clear inspiration for *Nightmare*'s aesthetic. Apples fall from trees and burst open to reveal squirming maggots similar to the insides of Oogie Boogie. Spooky tree branches grow from thin air with a twisted melancholy, just like Sally's burning thistle branch turns into a Christmas tree.

Švankmajer's style of combining live action with realistic creatures carried on through the late 1970s, when stop-motion animation technology moved forward at Will Vinton Studios in Portland and at George Lucas's special effects house, Industrial Light & Magic (ILM), in the San Francisco Bay Area. The practical creature animation done by Phil Tippett and his crew at ILM brought the holographic chess table aliens and tauntauns to life in *Star Wars: A New Hope* (1977) and *Star Wars: The Empire Strikes Back* (1980), respectively. In the 1990s, ILM and much of Hollywood fully embraced CGI after the release of *Jurassic Park* (1993). However, both *Tim Burton's The Nightmare Before Christmas* and Nick Park's short film *The Wrong Trousers*, released to much acclaim that same year, proved that stop-motion would be sticking around into the twenty-first century and beyond.

BELOW: Film poster for *Mad Monster Party?* (1967), the first stop-motion monster musical made by Rankin/Bass Productions.

CHAPTER 2

SETTING A *NIGHTMARE* INTO MOTION

"It's something Tim Burton taught me a long time ago, and it holds true: 'The biggest successes are films that look normal, with a normal story.' But who's interested in doing that? Certainly not him or myself."

—HENRY SELICK, *CORALINE* (2009) AND *WENDELL & WILD* (2022)

Although Tim Burton and Henry Selick grew up on opposite sides of the country, their inspiration for entering the world of animation was very similar: They were both raised on monster movies and the stop-motion work of Ray Harryhausen, and they had an unshakeable focus on creating art. Both Burton and Selick grew up being known, according to Selick, "as that weird kid that's drawing all the time." This outsider mentality shows up in nearly all of Burton and Selick's films—most notably the antihero Jack Skellington in *Tim Burton's The Nightmare Before Christmas*, who feels lost and out of place in his Halloween-themed world.

FROM CALARTS TO DISNEY

This common interest in all things scary brewed in Selick from a young age. Although he grew up in New Jersey, Selick says his penchant for macabre storytelling came from summers listening to ghost stories in Alabama and visiting his relatives in his mother's hometown. Following high school, Selick faced the choice of taking a musician's path or the artist's route. Although he was a lover of music and enjoyed playing in a rock band, Selick was also great at drawing and intrigued by the art of filmmakers like Reiniger and Harryhausen. Ultimately, he chose to study art at Syracuse University and Central Saint Martins College of Art and Design in London, and in 1977 he graduated with an MFA in experimental animation from the California Institute of the Arts (CalArts). This CalArts program was designed for students interested in innovative animation. It focused on developing each student's unique style, not mirroring the Disney greats, and the curriculum was looser than the character animation degree Tim Burton eventually earned at CalArts.

Burton grew up in suburbanized Burbank, California, with its cookie-cutter, brightly colored homes and warm, sunshiny weather. This might seem like an unfit birthplace for a horror aficionado with a knack for tinkering with the status quo, but Burton turned to art and filmmaking at a young age. After he won a competition to illustrate an anti-litter campaign, one of his drawings was featured on the side of Burbank garbage trucks. He also embraced the holiday season by painting neighbors' windows with decorations to earn extra cash.

Burton's early artistic endeavors paid off when he received a scholarship to CalArts. He recalls his college experience as an interesting time full of many different talented people coming together from several walks of life. The character animation program was designed to foster the traditional animation style, but inevitably, the young artists developed their own unique ideas. "The idea was that it was a foundation in Disney animation," Burton says. "But animators just like animation, so everybody had interests in different things."

PAGE 24: Concept art of Jack in the graveyard of Halloween Town.

LEFT: Tim Burton poses with screen-used puppets in the puppet fabrication department at Skellington Productions.

OPPOSITE LEFT: A young Tim Burton in a skeleton costume, handmade by his mother.

OPPOSITE RIGHT: Henry Selick, director of *Tim Burton's The Nightmare Before Christmas.*

Burton dazzled his fellow classmates with his 1979 animated short, *Stalk of the Celery Monster*. The film was certainly in the same vein as his beloved monster movies, like *Frankenstein* (1931) and *Dracula* (1931), and it focused on a mad scientist (really a dentist) not unlike Dr. Finkelstein in *Tim Burton's The Nightmare Before Christmas*. That short film also got Burton noticed by Disney, where shortly after graduation, he worked as an animator on *The Fox and the Hound* (1981). However, the movie's traditional Disney sweetness clashed with the filmmaker's more macabre aesthetic, and he found himself "very emotionally agitated" during his early years with the company. "I couldn't even fake the Disney style," Burton recalls of the foxes he was assigned to draw. "Mine looked like roadkills."

One Disney project that proved more Burton's style was titled *Trick or Treat*. Though it lacked a script, Disney was collecting art for a potential stop-motion film inspired by three elements: haunted houses, kids, and Halloween. The project never made it past Burton's scary illustrations, but one drawing of five well-dressed ghouls shows a strong resemblance to the street musicians in *Tim Burton's The Nightmare Before Christmas*.

KINDRED SPIRITS

Tim Burton's creative frustration while working for Disney was shared by fellow animator and kindred spirit Henry Selick. Selick joined Disney in 1977 as an "in-betweener," which is the animation term for the person who draws the frames in-between two important frames to create a smoother transition. It wasn't a glamorous role, but it eventually landed him a job alongside Burton animating on *The Fox and the Hound* (1981) under the supervision of Glen Keane. Selick, like Burton, also found little inspiration from drawing cute animals, and he experienced the same disappointment from contributing to shelved projects. Selick says of his early friendship with Burton: "In the art and film world, you find out that there are five people out there who are very much like yourself, and you're either going to work well together or hate each other and be jealous of one another. Fortunately, Tim Burton and I get along well; we share a lot of common interests."

By 1982, Burton was discouraged by his inability to create the quirky, scary art he loved and contemplated leaving Disney. He had completed two hundred pieces of concept art for the film *The Black Cauldron* (1985) that weren't used in the final film. Two Disney allies, screenwriter Julie Hickson and production executive Tom Wilhite, saw a unique talent in Burton from his previous work, and they gave him an opportunity to kick-start his career and fine-tune his macabre aesthetic with a new project.

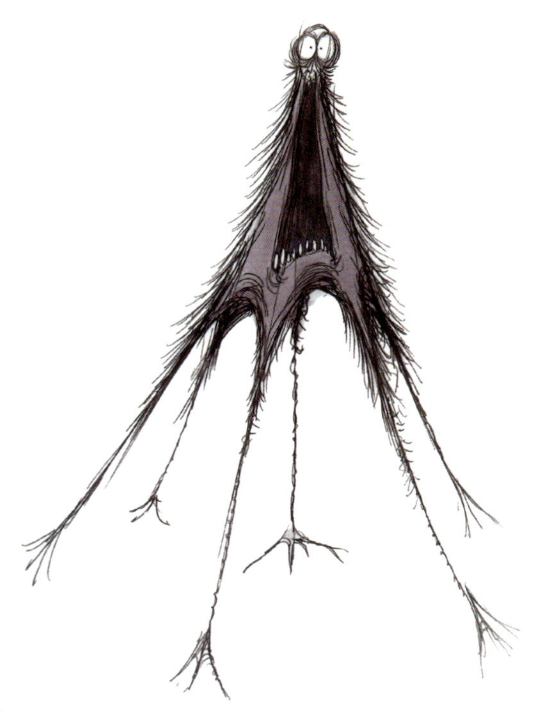

TOP AND BOTTOM: Tim Burton's concept art created for Disney's *The Black Cauldron* (1985). Unfortunately, Burton's designs were never used.

OPPOSITE TOP: A still from Disney's *The Fox and the Hound* (1981).

OPPOSITE BOTTOM: Tim Burton's doodle pad.

Vincent (1982) began as a poem Burton wrote in the style of one of his greatest inspirations, Dr. Seuss. It's a story about a quirky boy whose obsession with Vincent Price, the famed horror actor, permeates all aspects of his young life. Originally imagined as a children's book, Burton changed directions when Wilhite gave him 60,000 dollars to produce *Vincent* as a stop-motion test for the ultimately unproduced Disney project *Trick or Treat*. Stop-motion was a true passion for Burton, and creating an animated film based on a poem would allow for more detailed depictions of the main character's creepy antics.

"I wanted to do that kind of animation because I felt there was a gravity to those three-dimensional figures that was more real for that story. That was really important for me," Burton says. It was the perfect project to keep Burton busy at Disney for two more months.

Fellow Disney animator Rick Heinrichs, who later won the Academy Award for Best Production Design on *Sleepy Hollow* (1999), produced and contributed to the overall design of *Vincent*—establishing a long creative partnership with Burton that extended to *Tim Burton's The Nightmare Before Christmas* and beyond. Stop-motion animator

Stephen Chiodo (*Killer Klowns from Outer Space*, 1988) and cameraman Victor Abdalov also joined the project to create the seven-minute masterpiece, with perfectly fitting narration by Vincent Price himself.

Although the short film *Vincent* was a creative win for Burton, Disney studio was understandably unsure how to market the project—the short was very different in style and tone than other Disney films at this point. It received a short theatrical release and played alongside the coming-of-age drama *Tex* (1982) in just one Los Angeles theater. Despite the limited fanfare, *Vincent* still garnered acclaim at festivals both domestic and abroad, and it took home the Critic's Award at the Annecy festival in 1983.

A *NIGHTMARE* IS BORN

As Tim Burton wrapped up work on *Vincent*, he began sketching some designs for a poem he'd written titled "The Nightmare Before Christmas." The poem was a perfect blend of Seussian whimsy and rhythm, with all the makings of a classic holiday spoof of Clement C. Moore's "A Visit from St. Nicholas" (commonly known as "The Night Before Christmas"). Moore's poem, originally published on December 23, 1832, recounted the magic of Santa Claus visiting children's homes on Christmas Eve. In Burton's reworked version, Jack Skellington, who hails from a land called Halloween Town, takes over Santa's job with his trusty canine pal Zero but ultimately bungles the delivery of the Christmas presents. The poem iteration of Jack Skellington existed alongside a visual depiction of him as a gaunt, elegant skeleton, which Burton had been repeatedly sketching in his spare time.

"The Jack character just came out as a drawing," Burton remembers. "I was bored, so I would doodle things a lot. It was an image that kept coming up. I think it was about roughly the same time I wrote the poem, but it wasn't necessarily directly linked. It was one of those subconscious things. He was a character that I kept drawing, and it was all percolating roughly at the same time."

The filmmaker had a lifelong love of Christmas and Halloween, two holidays he often merged into one in his own celebrations. In writing the poem, he was inspired by Dr. Seuss as much as Moore's original—particularly the author's 1957 classic *How the Grinch Stole Christmas!* "I grew up loving Dr. Seuss," the filmmaker notes. "The rhythm of his stuff spoke to me very clearly. Dr. Seuss's books were perfect: the right number of words, the right rhythm, great subversive stories."

Originally, Burton had intended to publish "The Nightmare Before Christmas" as a children's book. He recalls taking it to nearly every publisher in New York City around the same time he was working on *The Black Cauldron*. Even though the publishers were captivated by the story, every publishing house passed. "I truly went almost everywhere and no one wanted it," Burton says. "At the time, I loved it, and I just wanted to get it published."

Undeterred, Burton shifted his focus to adapting the poem into a stop-motion holiday film similar to Rankin/Bass's *Rudolph the Red-Nosed Reindeer*, which first aired on television in 1964 and became an annual viewing tradition. He sketched concept artwork and storyboards expanding Jack's world and enlisted Rick Heinrichs to create a 3D model of Jack. The pair pitched the film to The Walt Disney Company as a stop-motion animated feature that would evoke both Halloween and Christmas.

"Stop-motion had a power over me and reality to it that felt right for this story," Burton says. "That's why I held out for it, because it was the right way to go. I always knew it, even though at the early stages someone had suggested to make a half-hour film. In fact, they even suggested making it a drawn animated special. But I couldn't do that because Jack felt too real to me. To me, stop-motion had the emotion and the realism that fit this material. And that's why it took so long to get it made."

Due to Burton's employment while creating the idea, Disney legally owned *Nightmare*, and Jack, Zero, and Santa Claus remained in the Disney vault through the 1980s. He completed two more half-hour-long projects while at Disney: a live-action version of the Grimms' fairy tale *Hansel and Gretel* (1983), which later aired on Disney Channel as part of the *Disney Studio Showcase* series, and a live-action, black-and-white short film starring Shelley Duvall and Daniel Stern titled *Frankenweenie* (1984), the predecessor to Burton's 2012 animated feature film of the same name. Similar to *Vincent* and his short films in college, *Frankenweenie* played to Burton's developing strengths: a peculiar young boy (played by Barret Oliver), a gothic motif, and a hat-tip to classic monster movies.

Burton and Selick both left Disney in the early 1980s. Burton succeeded as a director of hit feature films, such as *Pee-wee's Big Adventure* (1985), *Beetlejuice* (1988), *Batman* (1989), and *Edward Scissorhands* (1990), whereas Selick relocated to San Francisco to work on stop-motion interstitials for MTV and animated commercials featuring the Pillsbury Doughboy. Selick's experience working with a crew of animators would prove useful when the time came to assemble what was then the largest animation team ever for a stop-motion film.

OPPOSITE: Early sketches of Jack Skellington created by Tim Burton.

ABOVE AND TOP LEFT: Burton's original drawings of Jack Skellington.

TOP RIGHT: An original drawing of Jack Skellington, Sally, and Zero created by Tim Burton.

THE SKELETON HE COULDN'T SHAKE

In 1990, eight years after Tim Burton's initial sketches of Jack Skellington, he couldn't shake the project from his mind, so he asked his agent to inquire with Disney about the rights. Sure enough, Disney had ownership of Jack, Zero, and the whole concept, and they were now eager to collaborate with one of the hottest new directors in Hollywood.

Disney was not only receptive to working with Burton, but they were also supportive of his idea to create a feature-length film entirely in stop-motion. Despite his passion for the art form, Burton decided to pass on the role of director for two reasons: First, he was committed to a second *Batman* film that would certainly monopolize his time, and second, he wasn't naive to the commitment required of a stop-motion film of *any* length—let alone one with a run time of over an hour. Wanting his project to move forward, Burton knew someone else needed to occupy the director's chair, and he had the perfect person.

Conveniently, Henry Selick had already seen the sketches for *Nightmare* back in 1982, when the pair were still working at Disney. He recalls, "It was one of the most interesting projects I'd ever seen." The proposition came to Selick via Rick Heinrichs; at that point, there were three songs and a three-page poem, but no real script, giving Selick a chance to experiement. According to Burton, "Henry wasn't the Disney animator-type. He was much more experimental and used different mediums. Luckily, the timing worked out."

Although Burton's "Nightmare" originated as a fairly lengthy and descriptive poem, Burton knew the story needed to be fleshed out to work as a feature-length film. The poem featured only three characters: Jack Skellington, Zero, and Santa Claus, and it didn't have the full character arc required of a movie narrative. Initially, Burton tapped *Beetlejuice* screenwriter Michael McDowell to adapt the poem into a script, but that collaboration ultimately didn't work out. The filmmaker instead pivoted to collaborating with Danny Elfman, with whom he worked on several prior occasions, to make the film into a musical.

Alongside Burton, Elfman wrote several musical numbers, working from a story outline and a collection of sketches that detailed Jack's scheme to save Christmas after kidnapping Santa Claus. The pair drew on various influences, including Burton's long-held feelings of being a misfit and Elfman's personal experiences as the beloved leader of a rock band, Oingo Boingo, which he wanted to leave. Burton also pulled inspiration from the monster movies he'd loved as a child when imagining Jack, an unlikely hero.

LEFT: A frame of Jack while singing atop the Spiral Hill.

TOP: Tim Burton's drawing of Santa Jack with his pumpkin-nosed dog, Zero.

OPPOSITE TOP: Jack running into the gate after discovering Christmas Town.

OPPOSITE BOTTOM: Story sketch of Jack arriving in Christmas Town.

"He's the classic misunderstood monster," Burton explains. "I grew up watching monster movies, and I felt all monsters were actually not villains but the most emotional characters in the films, like Frankenstein's monster and King Kong. Every monster is perceived as the bad guy, but they're not that bad of a guy. They're tortured, they're misguided, but they're not bad people. Feeling how I did about Halloween and Christmas, with a certain opposite juxtaposition of those holidays, the story and the character came together based on a lot of feelings that I had about a lot of things. Jack was always very positive, very energetic, and very misguided. Jack is an optimistic character. He's something that's perceived as scary or bad, but he is truly just a good person and a positive, artistic person. That's why I always loved [director] Ed Wood, because it was like, 'He's horrible but passionate and cares about something even if it's garbage.' I've always identified with those types of characters."

Selick, a truly devout stop-motion animator and longtime friend of Burton, was happy to take on the challenge. He quickly got to work on the musical number, "What's This?", which Elfman had recorded as a demo, using storyboards by artist Joe Ranft for reference, to ensure there was no delay in the production. The filmmakers purposefully selected the most colorful, whimsical musical sequence to encourage more support from The Walt Disney Company and its offshoot Touchstone Pictures, which would distribute the film.

"Danny knew there had to be a scene where Jack Skellington discovers Christmas Town, so he wrote and recorded 'What's This?'," explained cinematographer Pete Kozachik. "That got us going. Joe Ranft and his guys churned out storyboards to illustrate the song, which fed production designer Deane Taylor and his assistants. Henry picked one shot out of the thirty-six shots boarded, shot number WHA-32. That would be the shot we'd begin the movie with."

Before any of that could happen, however, Selick needed to secure the right team of animators and the right location to make Burton's *Nightmare* a stop-motion reality.

CHAPTER 3

ASSEMBLING AN ANIMATION DREAM TEAM

"[*Nightmare*] was probably the only project that I've ever done where it felt very clear to me . . . and that's why I felt comfortable with Henry and these artists and all the other people coming onboard."

—TIM BURTON

When one imagines the city of San Francisco, one thinks of counterculture and cable cars, sourdough, and the Summer of Love. Very few people imagine what it really was in the late 1980s and early 1990s: a haven for stop-motion animators. In 1978, George Lucas brought his special effects studio, Industrial Light & Magic, from the Los Angeles area up to the Bay Area. Lucas brought stop-motion legend and Bay Area native Phil Tippett with him and built a real presence in the effects and animation fields. When it comes to filmmaking, San Francisco may always be overshadowed by Los Angeles, its neighbor down south, but this artsy city has maintained its own unique corner of the film industry for decades.

Perhaps one reason San Francisco has attracted the stop-motion crowd is its history as a home for the unique and off-kilter. Stop-motion, particularly in the days before digital editing software, is an almost maddening art form that requires a specific type of person. As animator Tim Hittle puts it, "One has to have the qualities of an oddball or a weirdo to be a stop-mo animator."

Tim Burton's The Nightmare Before Christmas delves into themes of identity, self-discovery, and the risks of imposing one's vision on the unfamiliar. Behind the scenes of the film is an equally captivating story—one of creative "oddballs and weirdos" uniting to craft a movie that was just as unique and unconventional as each and every one of them.

CREATING A CLAN OF WEIRDOS

In the late 1980s, two Bay Area production companies, Colossal Pictures and Premavision, brought animators from all over the country to Northern California. Colossal was producing stop-motion commercials featuring the likes of the Pillsbury Doughboy, Hershey Kisses, and Ritz Bits Crackers, as well as some shorts for MTV that Henry Selick was directing. In 1987, Art Clokey, creator of the original stop-motion series *The Gumby Show*, opened Premavision in Sausalito, California, just across the Golden Gate Bridge from San Francisco. Art and his wife, Gloria, set out to introduce the Gumby of the 1950s and 1960s to a new audience of kids with a whopping ninety-nine new episodes called *Gumby Adventures*.

Within these two production companies, much of the future animation team of *Tim Burton's The Nightmare Before Christmas* was found. "Gumby was the great training ground we all learned on," says animator Owen Klatte. "Our first stuff looked terrible because we didn't know what we were doing at all hardly, but it went on TV anyway. We learned so much."

Production on *Gumby Adventures* wrapped in 1988, leaving many of the animators without a clear next step. Selick encouraged many of them to join Colossal to help animate the Pillsbury Doughboy, and the close-knit crew continued to work on TV spots together—until the director had bigger projects for them to tackle.

Animation supervisor Eric Leighton and animators Trey Thomas and Owen Klatte were among the first members of the *Nightmare* animation crew. All three had worked on *Gumby Adventures* at Premavision and eventually assisted Selick with his personally written and directed TV short, *Slow Bob in the Lower Dimensions* (1991). *Slow Bob* was the surreal, nightmarish pilot for a show that would have aired on MTV . . . had Selick not been asked to join forces with Burton. The short took

PAGE 34: Jack Skellington exploring Christmas Town.

BELOW: Animators Angie Glocka and Trey Thomas behind a sign featuring the film's title.

home an award at the 1992 Ottawa International Animation Festival, as well as praise from Burton, who greatly admired Selick's work with MTV.

Three more *Gumby Adventures* alumni joined the crew, including Mike Belzer, who had also done work with Selick at Colossal Pictures; Tim Hittle, whose animated short *The Potato Hunter* (1991) won the Best Short award at the Seattle International Film Festival; and Angie Glocka, who had done some commercial work after moving to California from her home state of Wisconsin. Glocka also happened to be married to fellow animator Owen Klatte, and so the crew now had their sole female animator and an artistic powerhouse of a couple to boot. "I will admit I felt on top of the world being the only woman, I won't lie," Glocka recalls. "I learned from my dad, who taught me how to use the darkroom, and also a lot about building and power tools. It was very empowering."

In January 1992, Anthony Scott was next to join the team, rounding out the original seven animators. Scott was waiting to read a script before joining, something that is very standard on most films. On *Nightmare*, however, the script wouldn't materialize until well after the animators were already hard at work on the Christmas Town scenes. Composer Danny Elfman had written the song "What's This?", and it was all they needed to start developing their style and proving to Disney that the film would be visually stunning and unlike anything anyone had seen in stop-motion before.

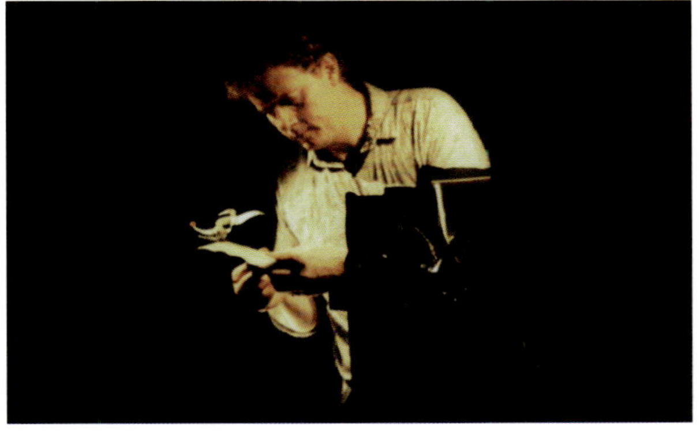

TOP: Tim Burton's sketch of the characters in Halloween Town, including Jack Skellington, Sally, Zero, the Mayor, a Vampire, the Wolfman, and the Corpse Kid.

LEFT: Animator Owen Klatte working with Zero.

FINDING A HOME

Obviously, for any animation to take place, the animators needed a playground, and the building that eventually housed "Skellington Productions" became a true home away from home for around 160 crew members: artists, animators, builders, camera people, and a very capable production management team. At first, Henry Selick had a short-lived home within Tippett Studio in Berkeley. Selick had made his MTV shorts there, but Phil Tippett was beginning work on an epic dinosaur project with Steven Spielberg (what became *Jurassic Park*). Tippett Studio was not big enough for that *and* Burton's stop-motion feature debut, and Selick and the early supervisors wondered: Could they find a studio in the Bay Area big enough to accommodate the grand scope of their vision?

They could—in San Francisco's South of Market district in the former San Francisco Studios building. Wander past 375 7th Street today and you'd never know what magic was created there more than thirty years ago. Though in fairness, the location during the production of *Nightmare* was just as discreet. In 1991, the building's only defining exterior feature was a few handprints in the cement sidewalk. The prints featured popular stars of the 1970s and 1980s like Whoopi Goldberg and Hervé Villechaize—like San Francisco's own little version of Hollywood-based Grauman's Chinese Theatre (or TCL Chinese Theatre, as it is now known). Today, the building has been replaced by Bessie Carmichael Elementary School and filled with children whose own parents might not have been old enough to see *Nightmare* when it first came to theaters.

ABOVE: The San Francisco Studios building, which would become the location of Skellington Productions.

In early summer 1991, Selick, along with producer Kathleen Gavin and some of the recently hired department heads, met to tour the potential filming location. The 40,000-square-foot film studio—with offices, stages, a set-building shop, screening room, and even garaged parking—was a unanimous hit. San Francisco Studios was renamed Skellington Productions, and the film crew moved in for the next several years.

The studio itself has been described as rickety, drafty, and altogether mazelike. Due to San Francisco's odd weather, even in summer the fog often made the building so cold it required bundling up. During production, one crew member recalls wearing long underwear to work every day until the windows were better sealed. Despite its flaws, the building was perhaps a perfect fit for a unique crew working on a groundbreaking movie, as it had an interesting layout that could accommodate the crew's evolving needs.

Inside the main entrance was a Ping-Pong table and a stairway. The Ping-Pong table was a great place to blow off steam after a tough shot, and the production hosted an ongoing tournament. Meanwhile, halfway up the staircase was painted the old industry phrase "Above the Line." This refers to a long-held film industry distinction about crew member roles: Those who work "above the line" include the production leadership—like the director, producer, and management—along with the screenwriter and cast (in *Nightmare*'s case, the voice actors). Below the line is everyone else.

The saying actually arose from the way film budgets were once tracked. The top sheet was used to list all the expenses related to the director, producer, story rights, and so on. These were totaled up, and below that line were the expenses for the rest of the crew and general production costs. In the case of Skellington Productions, the building itself divided the above- and below-the-line crew members, because the staircase led up to the offices of Selick, Gavin, and the art and story departments. To prevent any disconnect among the crew, Gavin scheduled one hour twice a week to walk around the studio and check in with everyone in every department. This nice gesture created a bridge between all parts of production, and many crew members still comment on Gavin's warmth and approachability today.

The bottom floor of Skellington Productions held what was known as "the bowling alley," which was a long walkway where the sets were stored. Also on the ground floor was a set of stairs that became a makeshift "green room" or hangout area for the crew members as they took breaks between filming. Here, animators would smoke a cigarette (which was still allowed indoors) or grab a soda and vent about a particular puppet that was giving them trouble (see "Top Five Tricky Puppets," page 108). Getting to the fabrication department required traveling through multiple areas, and the mold-making and set-building areas were divided by a makeshift wall created by the set builders themselves. This scrappiness was also evident in the building's second machine shop, which was

BELOW TOP: Camera operator Jo Carson and assistant camera Jim Matlosz on the set of Halloween Town.

BELOW BOTTOM: Making Christmas.

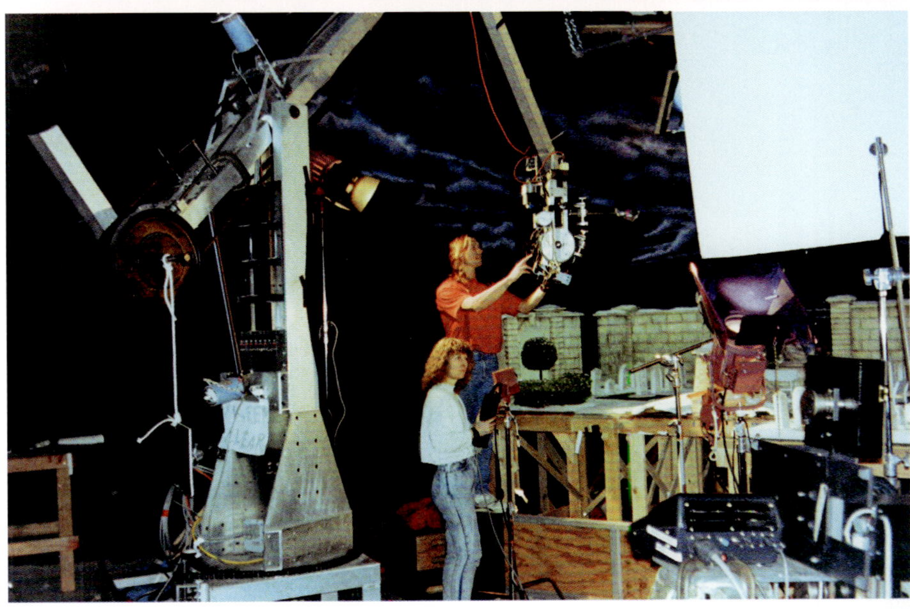

ABOVE: Concept art of Lock, Shock, and Barrel.

OPPOSITE TOP: Animator Tim Hittle working with Jack and Sally on the Spiral Hill set.

OPPOSITE BOTTOM: The Pumpkin King's flames were added to the film during postproduction.

just a storage unit added to the front of the building by armature builder Chris Rand.

The studio had multiple shooting stages: Some were small, like the one used for the "Poor Jack" sequence, and some were large and housed bigger sets like Town Hall. The biggest stage was divided into multiple stages that were separated by black duvetyne curtains. The stages were the quietest areas of the entire building, eliminating distractions for the animators who needed to maintain deep concentration to do their work. The only interruption was the PA system, which could be heard throughout the whole building.

As production continued and the needs of the crew evolved, the studio changed along with them. The convenient parking garage, which hosted one particularly amazing Halloween party, was eventually transformed into more stages. Yet, despite shifting priorities and the always impending deadlines, the general camaraderie between crew members never dimmed. The studio was a constant bright spot for everyone. As Tim Burton says, "The studio was incredible, and I just loved going up there because that level of artistry and detail was magical, truly magical, and I'd never really felt that before."

WRITE ON TIME

BELOW: Caroline Thompson, writer for *Tim Burton's The Nightmare Before Christmas.*

OPPOSITE TOP: Story sketch from the musical number "Jack's Lament."

OPPOSITE BOTTOM LEFT: Detail from story sketch of Jack removing his head, from the musical number "Jack's Lament."

OPPOSITE BOTTOM RIGHT: Shot breakdown of Jack and Sally's duet in the cemetery.

By July 1991, even while Henry Selick shot some test footage at Tippett Studio in Berkeley, put together his crew, and moved the filmmakers into their new San Francisco studio in San Francisco, there was still no actual screenplay—and the work needed to begin in earnest.

While Elfman wrote the songs, he was living with then-partner Caroline Thompson, the screenwriter of Burton's *Edward Scissorhands*, who became instrumental in shaping the characters and narrative of *Tim Burton's The Nightmare Before Christmas*. Because Thompson was already familiar with the overall story and the characters, the studio asked if she would come on board to write the script at the same time production was kicking off. It was a somewhat backward process . . . and it took a character not even in Burton's original poem to help convince Thompson to do it.

"Danny had really told the whole story in song," she remembers. "If you pull the songs out, they tell an entire tale. So, I said, 'Well, I'll think about it.' Sally had to be redesigned for me to come in, and a couple of images came to me. One was her throwing herself out of the tower, and because she was stitched together, it gave me like a Frankenstein image. I saw all of her limbs falling and then I saw her back together again. The other image that came to me was her detaching her leg and leaving it for Oogie Boogie while she went to free Santa on the other side of the cave. Having those two images, I was comfortable saying, 'Okay, I'll take a crack at it.'"

Thompson went to visit the animators and crew at Skellington Productions, where she saw dozens of sketches and storyboards. Her goal was to flesh out the characters and to create a story arc that existed outside of Elfman's songs. After seeing a sketch of Dr. Finkelstein removing the top of his head and scratching his brain, she had the idea to create a subplot about the scientist as Sally's creator and Sally's eventual plan to escape him. Following her visit to the studio, Thompson and Elfman took a trip to a resort in Northern California where she wrote the screenplay in a week. The first draft of the script, dated August 5, 1991, was the only draft. It arrived just in time.

"Caroline is a talented writer and sort of pieced things together as Danny continued writing great songs," Selick remembers. "There are definitely some rose-colored glasses looking backward at all this. It wasn't easy. But I really think it was just fun and blind faith that kept us going, so we never got too down. As we went along, I was so interested in finding out about Jack and who he was. There was a sweetness and an insanity to him that I loved. You wanted to be carried along with the story. At the end of the day, the film is about that character and instantly connecting with him and wanting to see how things are going to work out."

Alongside Thompson's screenplay and Elfman's songs, Selick and his crew drew inspiration from a number of sources, both thematically and visually. Earlier films like Czech surrealist animator Jan Švankmajer's 1971 work *Jabberwocky* and Roy Rowland's 1953 film *The 5,000 Fingers of Dr. T.*, based on a story by Dr. Seuss, impacted the storytelling. Other influences included Charles Laughton's *The Night of the Hunter* (1955), Terry Gilliam's *The Adventures of Baron Munchausen* (1988), and Robert Wiene's *The Cabinet of Dr. Caligari* (1920).

"I've always said that Tim and I are from the same planet, just not the same neighborhood," Selick recalls. "So, I was building a style based on my inspirations, which included Tim. We drew much more from live-action films and illustrators and artists and so forth because there just weren't that many stop-motion films done in the style that we were going to be working in."

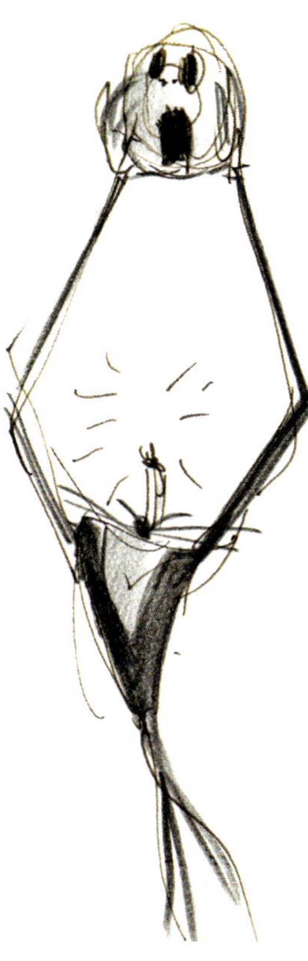

Although the film came to fruition in an unusual way, with the story and the songs being crafted before the actual script, the result is a compelling tale about two misfits who find belonging and, eventually, love. It reflects the inspirations of both Thompson and Elfman, whose contributions came together to create Sally and Jack. Although Jack is the protagonist, the emotional heft of the story relies on Sally as well.

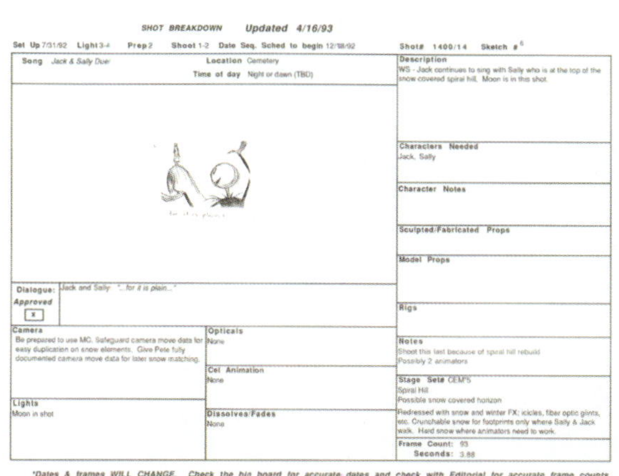

SHOT BREAKDOWN Updated 4/16/93

Set Up 7/31/92 Light 3-4 Prep 2 Shoot 1-2 Date Seq. Sched to begin 12/18/92 Shot# 1400/14 Sketch # 6

Song: Jack & Sally Duet
Location: Cemetery
Time of day: Night or dawn (TBD)

Description: WS - Jack continues to sing with Sally who is at the top of the snow covered spiral hill. Moon is in this shot.

Characters Needed: Jack, Sally

Character Notes

Sculpted/Fabricated Props

Model Props

Dialogue: Jack and Sally "...for it is plain..."
Approved [x]

Rigs

Camera: Be prepared to use MC. Safeguard camera move data for easy duplication on snow elements. Give Pete fully documented camera move data for later snow matching.

Opticals: None

Cel Animation: None

Notes: Shoot this last because of spiral hill rebuild. Possibly 2 animators

Stage Set# CEMP5
Spiral Hill
Possible snow covered horizon
Redressed with snow and winter FX; icicles, fiber optic glints, etc. Crunchable snow for footprints only where Sally & Jack walk. Hard snow where animators need to work.

Lights: Moon in shot

Dissolves/Fades: None

Frame Count: 93
Seconds: 3.88

*Dates & frames WILL CHANGE. Check the big board for accurate dates and check with Editorial for accurate frame counts.

"I'm proud that I was able to knit some coherence into something that could have really gone south," Thompson says. "I was able to find a supporting story to carry the narrative. Sally's story carries the movie in terms of narrative, and Jack's story carries the movie in terms of song. And Sally accomplishes a great thing. She humanizes Jack. She gives him a dimension he didn't otherwise have and humanizes him."

BECOMING A TEAM

With the songs completed, a studio located, and a screenplay in place, it was time to achieve the magic that Tim Burton desired. To do that, Henry Selick and Eric Leighton needed to set the bar extremely high for the team's animators. The animators were handed puppets of a higher quality than most of them had ever worked with before (see "Armatures," page 74), and they utilized more advanced tools to track their shot progress and had the luxury of doing several test shots before hopping into the final "hero shot." To top it off, director of photography Pete Kozachik's motion-control rigs allowed for the kind of cinematic camera movements that were never attempted in a simple stop-motion TV spot. It was clear early on that there was little room for error. The pace would be grueling to hit the film's release deadline.

To keep up with production's tight schedule, more animators were brought in to bring the total count to around nineteen. Among them was Paul Berry, an impressive English animator who created the stop-motion short film *The Sandman* (1991), which was nominated for a 1993 Academy Award. Berry also suggested his good friend Loyd Price, an animator who had spent eight years working on children's series for Cosgrove Hall Films in Manchester, England. "I was flown over to San Francisco for an interview and to do an animation test," says Price. "I remember the supervising animator, Eric Leighton, showing me some of the rushes, and I was absolutely amazed, as I'd never seen such good stop-motion animation before." Other animators included Joel Fletcher and Justin Kohn, who had worked for LA's Churchill Films; Stephen "Buck" Buckley and Richard Zimmerman, who both had worked on *Gumby Adventures*; and assistant animator Mike Johnson, who later codirected *Tim Burton's Corpse Bride* (2005). "[Stop-motion] requires, in my opinion, quite an artist and a technician, and that's a hard combination to find," Burton says.

Hard to find they certainly were. Only a small pool of stop-motion animators existed in the early 1990s, and ads were placed in newspapers all over the United States, Canada, and Europe to find this unique brand of artist. "Usually, you do stop-motion for a one-minute commercial," noted producer Denise Di Novi, who ran Tim Burton Productions at the time. "But we needed to build a whole studio from scratch. And we had to comb the world for animators." Producer Kathleen Gavin recalls, "Animators were our scarcest resource. It's very hard to find animators who can do work at this level." However, this scarcity later allowed the team to continue reuniting throughout their careers, as most of them hopped between gigs together.

Long nights on the set paired with a shared understanding of stop-motion minutiae created strong bonds and a creative aura that members of other departments noticed. "There was an energy around that group. It's very unique; very few people can do it; and when [they] all get together, that energy just amplifies," explains set builder Todd Lookinland. "There were a lot of problems to

ABOVE TOP: Animator Tim Hittle works with his favorite puppet, Jack.

ABOVE BOTTOM: The cake served at the *Nightmare* wrap party.

OPPOSITE LEFT: Animator Angie Glocka animates Timmy, a young resident of the Real World.

OPPOSITE RIGHT: The residents of Halloween Town behind the scenes.

solve and there was no reference book to look them up in. We had to figure out, 'How are we going to do this?' That makes it a really fun environment because you have to get creative and figure it out, whether it's a camera technique or a material that you're going to use to build something or a painting technique. There was no handbook on this movie. We just made it all up as we went along."

Angie Glocka shares the same sentiment: "You know how artists are! They often occupy a plane a little bit 'tweaked' and just to the left of center of the general population. So, you get a mass of them together, and it creates a unique universe. Plus, with Tim and Henry, there is that esoteric influence coming from the top."

The entire crew—ranging from the story department to puppet fabrication, from armature builders to set designers—has remarked on the closeness of the team. There was a strong sense of responsibility to make a great film, but at the same time, the predominantly young crew was lighthearted, despite most never having worked on a feature film before—let alone with a name like Tim Burton. There was a youthful, creative energy that ran through the studio. Several of them spent their evenings out at concerts in San Francisco and showed up to work on motorcycles. Some recall feeling like misfits and outcasts themselves, a connection to the film's story that resonated with those making it.

"A lot of us were young punks and listened to loud music and went out every night," recalls the film's production coordinator, Kat Alioshin. "Here was this scary-looking, dark story. We reacted with, 'Oh, yes, we're gonna love working on this.' Because every other film seemed to be so happy and lighthearted, and this was an intense, coming-of-age story of Jack trying to figure out what he wanted to do with his life. We all related to him."

"We had a lot of fun," adds associate producer Phil Lofaro. "Everybody was pretty young. We had a lot of tattooed, pierced biker types. You know, it was San Francisco, and so it had an outlaw feel to it. And that was fun."

Impressive parties were thrown, competitive tournaments were held, and even crew members' partners became great friends. One clear demonstration of this bond is shown in the heartfelt detail of Santa Jack's Christmas list. The names of the girls and boys on the list were actually the children of crew members, including Eric Leighton and production coordinator Jill Ruzicka's son, Oliver, and Buckley's daughter, Allison. "It was a family," Mike Belzer recalls. "It really was. Everybody working together, and I would say it was the best film that I've ever worked on. For sure. It was a magical, magical time."

STORIES FROM THE SET

Many of the animators and artists on *Tim Burton's The Nightmare Before Christmas* share some amazing stories—the good, the bad, and the hilarious—that could probably be a book all on their own.

ANGIE GLOCKA: "We always had intense deadlines and late hours, and I happened to animate the scene of Jack going up the chimney actually on Christmas Eve. I think I was the only one left on the stage that night, and I finished at 10 p.m., just after Jack's Santa hat cleared the chimney. So, there's Christmas energy embedded in the actual scene. Couldn't have been happier!"

ANTHONY SCOTT: "Tim Burton was busy with *Batman Returns* (1992) and *Ed Wood* (1994) while we were animating *Nightmare*. However, he did visit Skellington Productions a few times. One day, while I was working on the 'Poor Jack' sequence, someone from production informed me that Tim Burton wanted to stop by my set. I had never met him before, so I was a little stunned and surprised. He popped in and told me he really liked what I was doing with Jack in the sequence, how expressive he was. He spent some time looking at the set and then left. It was a quick visit, but it gave me a huge boost."

LOYD PRICE: "One of the things I really remember was when Paul Berry was animating the shot of Jack as the Pumpkin King setting himself on fire. Henry [Selick] and the director of photography, Pete Kozachik, wanted a live-action plate of the fire to project onto the puppet as Paul animated the shot. To get the acting right, they asked Paul to wave around a flaming torch in front of a greenscreen while they filmed it, not using stuntmen for this shot! The crew were there with fire extinguishers and blankets in case Paul caught on fire from any stray sparks, which was a real possibility, as Paul had hair that he used to spike up with a lot of hairspray. Fortunately for everyone concerned, nothing went wrong, and Paul did a great take that was then used as a plate in the film . . . but I'm pretty certain that he only did one!"

OPPOSITE: *The Nightmare Before Christmas* animation crew. Front row (left to right): Kim Blanchette, Timothy Hittle, Angie Glocka, Paul W. Jessel, and Loyd Price. Middle row (left to right): Paul Berry, Justin Kohn, Rich Zim, Eric Leighton, Joel Fletcher, and Mike Belzer. Back row (left to right): Harry Walton, Anthony Scott, Owen Klatte, and Trey Thomas.

MIKE BELZER: "I only had a few shots with Sally, and just speaking bluntly, she was a pain in the ass. Just very difficult. But I remember talking to Tim [Hittle] one time. I was like, 'Tim! Help me out, man, how do you get such good stuff out of Sally? She just fights me.' And he's just smoking a cigarette and he goes, 'Belz, you gotta treat her like a lady, you know? If you fight with her, she's gonna fight you back. Just love her. Just give her love, talk to her softly, and just give her the respect and love that she deserves, and she'll treat you right.' So fast-forward, I'm doing a Sally shot, and sure enough she's kicking my butt and nobody's around, and I'm looking around just like, okay, this is kind of crazy but . . . 'All right, Sally, it's just you and me, girl. Can you give me a little help here?' I kid you not, that shot went like butter after that."

OWEN KLATTE: "One of the wonderful things about *Nightmare* is how 'old school' it is, using hundred-year-old techniques with almost every visual effect shot in camera rather than comped in later or done through computer graphics. My favorite story related to that involves a rusty nail. During 'Oogie Boogie's Song,' some slot machines roll forward and fire guns and we see muzzle flashes. Well, when each gun got animated to the position at which it needed to fire, the camera operator would rewind the camera. I'd drape black velvet around my arms and climb up onto the set. I'd hold a rusty nail next to the tip of the gun and press a Dremel tool to the nail to create sparks. The black velvet would keep me from being seen on the final shot, and those sparks would be double exposed over the animation to create the muzzle flashes. I don't know who came up with that brilliantly simple and effective idea, but I love it."

TIM HITTLE: "My favorite scene I animated is the end of the film. Sally walks up the hill and sits with her flower. Jack approaches, and they sing to one another as he slowly walks up to be with her. Everything worked together beautifully—music, set, lighting, camera, and animation. It was one of those rare times when I just knew what to do and what I wanted, and I had the skill and experience to pull it off. All things came together for me at that time shooting those shots. I am still moved when I see it after all this time."

WHAT DOES IT TAKE TO BE AN ANIMATOR?

ANGIE GLOCKA: "Patience! Number one quality. In those days, an excellent memory was also paramount, since we couldn't play back and view our entire shot. One had to hold the entire scene in one's head. Also, nerves of steel, in a way."

ANTHONY SCOTT: "It takes someone who pays close attention to detail and doesn't mind spending days or weeks to produce a few seconds."

JOEL FLETCHER: "The most important characteristic for stop-motion animators is a passion and love of the art form. Attention to detail, patience, and stamina are also crucial. Animators need to be an astute observer of how things move, as well as how to give an acting performance through a puppet. The actual act of stop-motion requires sustained focus for long periods of time. This is commonly called 'being in the zone,' or the high-level state known as 'flow.' These are the peculiar traits that stop-motion animators have in common."

LOYD PRICE: "Everyone always says that you must have so much patience to be an animator, which is true, but to be honest, if you didn't have this, you wouldn't go into animating anyway, as it would be so frustrating. An animator, especially a stop-motion animator, is really an actor who does their acting scenes in slow motion. Something that might only take fifteen seconds to shoot in live action can take days or even weeks, and you have to maintain your level of focus and concentration so that you don't make a technical mistake or lose the acting focus of the shot. So, the ability to focus and concentrate for long periods of time is absolutely crucial. You also have to have a very good eye for spatial awareness to see the increments that you are animating and the ability to bend and contort your body into positions to be able to access the puppets on the sets!"

OWEN KLATTE: "Animation, in general, requires a certain kind of patience and attention to detail. Stop-motion, though, has to be shot progressively one frame after another, without being able to work with key frames or adjusting in-betweens later on. It is a kind of ultra-slow-motion performance that has to be done right the first time or redone from scratch. So, you need to have a very high level of concentration, enjoy staying in a creative zone for long periods of time, and be happy working alone in a dark room for hours on end."

TIM HITTLE: "I think one has to have the qualities of an oddball or a weirdo to be a stop-mo animator. It involves spending so many hours alone doing painstaking work. But beauty can be achieved with the work and it is worthwhile. Some of the best people are oddballs and weirdos."

BOTTOM LEFT: A Halloween Town resident's creation and Jack Skellington playing as Santa Jack, by Tim Burton.

OPPOSITE: Art and details from Tim Burton's original poem, *The Nightmare Before Christmas*.

BE PREPARED FOR LONG DAYS AND SETBACKS

ANGIE GLOCKA: "On one of the experiment scenes—I think it was the "Cutting Open the Teddy Bear" scene—I had left maybe four surface gauges [see page 101] in position in the middle of shooting my test so I could go to lunch. When I returned, someone from camera had removed all my gauges so they could do some additional camera tweaking. Apparently, the spindles were poking them as they worked, and they didn't realize that the gauges were in position. Luckily, it was only a test. I just swallowed hard, said nothing, and proceeded to set up the shot all over again, adding an additional two hours to my already long day. These were the times when I reminded myself, 'Lucky to be here, lucky to be here, lucky to be here . . .'"

BUCK BUCKLEY: "When leaving the studio, usually late at night, the last thing an animator does is take a light meter reading. It's an old-school way to keep the lighting consistent on a shot that might take several days. Say it's 2 a.m., I always liked working late and alone. You feel tender, and there is always a cold breeze blowing through the stages . . . It's the ghosts around, keeping it real!"

JOEL FLETCHER: "I worked a lot of overtime. Depending on the complexity and length of the shot, it would take anywhere from two to five days or more to complete. Stop-motion takes a lot of sustained mental focus, and the expected standards were very high, which was quite stressful."

LOYD PRICE: "Working on *Nightmare* was very demanding. The hours were really long as we were doing twelve-hour days for months on end, but you knew that you were really creating something magical, so you went all-in to do it. The hardest thing for me, personally, was that I'd left my wife and three young children back in England, as we knew that the working hours would be so long on the film. My youngest daughter, Rosy, was only two weeks old when I went over to San Francisco, and I only saw them twice, for a week each time, during the nine months that I worked on the film. This was before the internet, so I spent a fortune on phone calls back home!"

MIKE BELZER: "I often call stop-motion 'the improvisation of animation' because you have puppets that have their own mind, I swear. You think you're gonna go this way with it, and all of a sudden, it's not working. You're not going to break the puppet, so you kinda do something on the fly. It's a dance between you and the puppet."

OWEN KLATTE: "We were all pushing ourselves, and being pushed to create something great, so to this day I consider *Nightmare* to be the hardest job I ever had. Long hours, intense pressure, but well worth it!"

RIGHT: A sketch of Lock, Shock, and Barrel by Tim Burton.

OPPOSITE TOP: Santa Jack flies away into the night, led by his skeletal reindeer.

OPPOSITE BOTTOM: Set builders Phil Brotherton (left) and Todd Lookinland (right) in front of a Halloween Town set.

CHAPTER 4

GETTING INTO CHARACTER

"There's a camera, and there's an animator, and there's a puppet, and nothing comes between them. You feel that human hands touched this, and an artist expressed this."

—MARK GUSTAFSON, GUILLERMO DEL TORO'S *PINOCCHIO* (2022)

If you've watched any movie by Tim Burton—say, *Beetlejuice*, *Corpse Bride*, *Edward Scissorhands*, and so on—you know that quirky, unique, even unsettling characters are a key ingredient of each film's appeal. Particularly in his animated films, his style shines through the design of each character, making them easily recognizable and often imitated. Their exaggerated features—deep-set, heavily shaded eyes, spindly limbs, and gothic-inspired wardrobes—make his characters seem like they have climbed right out of Burton's sketchbook and onto the big screen.

Every character in Burton's stop-motion films is a carefully crafted puppet with a sturdy skeleton and a meticulous design. It takes weeks of work by talented teams of designers, armature builders, and fabricators to make these inanimate figures appear as human as any living, breathing actor. The characters of *Tim Burton's The Nightmare Before Christmas* have unique stories and personalities that are made richer and more believable through each coat of paint, swatch of fabric, and carefully positioned strand of hair.

1A
Rev.

3B
Rev

WHOA
3D
Rev.

MAY.

8
Rev.

CHARACTER DEVELOPMENT

What's a fantastical world without vibrant, compelling inhabitants? Tim Burton's original poem centered on only three characters: Jack Skellington, his pet dog Zero, and a specific iteration of Santa Claus. To translate the poem to the big screen, the filmmakers needed to populate Halloween Town with lively and sometimes horrific characters, from Sally to Oogie Boogie to the town's two-faced Mayor. As Jack discovers his purpose on a journey from Halloween Town to Christmas Town and back again, he encounters friends, foes, and family along the way. Despite their horrific appearances, none of the characters in *Tim Burton's The Nightmare Before Christmas* are intended to be evil. Instead, they highlight our common misconceptions about those who appear to be misfits.

"Here you have this story where there are no *really* bad characters, not even Oogie Boogie," according to Burton. "He's not really bad; he's just the weird neighbor in this weird city. And you have this character, Jack, who just wants to do good; he's passionate about something, and basically, he ends up being misperceived and scaring everybody."

Though the film centers on several lead characters, with Jack at the forefront of the story, the filmmakers and animators needed to fill the story with background characters who matched Burton's original vision. Early on in production, Burton gave a few original sketches to the art department to work with for character design. These included characters like Jack, Sally, Zero, and Santa Claus, along with other sketches that were random doodles pulled from the pages of Burton's sketchbooks.

Rick Heinrichs and the art department looked at Burton's sketches and drawings for inspiration, but also conceived characters who felt right for the film's terrifying but endearing aesthetic.

"In the town meeting, you see a lot of incidental characters, so we had to come up with ideas for that," Heinrichs remembers. "The witches and the vampires and the little kid with a sewn-up eye. There was a melting man—that was Tim's concept. I did a sculpture of him using wax that was really melting."

PAGE 52: Concept art of Lock, Shock, and Barrel, ready to kidnap Santa Claus.

OPPOSITE: Story sketches of the Mayor announcing the search for Jack Skellington to the residents of Halloween Town.

RIGHT: Drawing of Sally by assistant art director Kendal Cronkhite.

TOP: Sketches of the vampires.

OPPOSITE: Tim Burton's drawing of Jack and Zero with Santa Claus.

The vampires in particular have become a fan favorite. In the film, four caped vampires appear, each with his own personality and body shape. Heinrichs pulled from one of Burton's 1980 sketches for the abandoned *Trick or Treat* to create the bloodsuckers. "The vampires appear only briefly and have funny-sounding, high voices," Heinrichs says. "There was something about the way Tim depicted them that felt more real as a vampire than almost any other screen version of them. He somehow caught both the human and the animal quality, and it was funny at the same time. That's what Tim brings to all of his depictions of character by walking the line between the horror and humor—there's something that feels very organic to the characters' essence in what he draws."

Each character had to be designed and built by the crew to help them feel as real as possible. Because the film was stop-motion, the characters were constructed as puppets with armature skeletons that allowed them to be moved millimeter by millimeter to create the sense of movement. Once they were built, they were decorated, painted, and dressed in costume. Several of the characters, including Jack and Sally, had removable heads or faces to allow them to change expression. After that, it was up to the animators to make each one feel alive on-screen, matching the motion and gestures to the voice cast's recordings. It was an involved process that ultimately allowed each character in the film to feel like a living, breathing person—or creature—who has a backstory and hopes for the future.

THIS SPREAD: Concept art of the various residents of Halloween Town.

JACK SKELLINGTON

Jack Skellington, the Pumpkin King of Halloween Town, is a dapper, energetic figure who is also grappling with some deep existential questions. He is disheartened by the same Halloween celebrations year after year, and he assumes that adventure will be found away from his community of Halloween Town.

"Jack is like a lot of characters in classic literature who are passionate and have a desire to do something in a way that isn't really acknowledged, just like that *Don Quixote* story, in which some character is on a quest for some sort of feeling, not even knowing what that is," Tim Burton said. "It's a very primal thing to me, that kind of searching for something and not even knowing what it is but being passionate about it. There are just aspects to the character of Jack that I like and identify with. It means something to me."

The character was also inspired by Danny Elfman, who was the lead singer of Oingo Boingo at the time. "Jack was an extension of what I was feeling at the time," he explained. "A lead singer in a band is like a king of their own little world, but I was at the point where I didn't want to be in a band anymore. I was writing from my own heart. He's got all these fans and people love him, but he's not happy."

It's somewhat ironic that, just as Jack tries to fill dual roles in *Nightmare*—as the Pumpkin King and as Santa Jack—it took a duo to fill the role of Jack. Elfman recorded Jack's musical numbers and provided his singing voice. "[Jack's] enthusiasm was really contagious," he recalls. "I really got into it, and I really began to like going from the ups and downs and the highs and lows and being able to really stretch the voice around. It was so much fun."

Meanwhile, actor Chris Sarandon was cast as Jack's speaking voice, which is confident and has a specific rhythmic cadence. "There was a very clear pathway into the sound of the character both from hearing Danny singing and also from the visuals that I was provided," Sarandon remembers. "I recall Henry Selick and I talked about it a bit, but then we jumped right into it. We didn't talk deeply about the character because Jack's journey and how you have to get there are built into the script. And then we tried everything. It was very creative because I was allowed all sorts of choices reading the lines."

From a visual perspective, Jack as a ghoulish skeleton, with hollow eyes, a bat-like bow tie, and lanky, suit-covered limbs, was the original look that Burton intended. "Tim puts down his idea and pretty much doesn't change it," says Rick Heinrichs, who sculpted the first 3D model of Jack. "But I was told by one of the armature builders that the legs were too skinny for them to build a practical joint within—Tim had just used a pen line for the legs, and it was very thin. It was interesting to engage in that dialogue of the aesthetic versus the practical. Because stop-motion is all about what's practical in order to create the magical effect of it. It's real objects in real life, and Jack has an enormous amount of charm because of all the life the animators put into him."

It often wasn't easy for the animators to give Jack that much-needed life, due to his noticeable lack of eyeballs—a daring choice, especially in animation. Emotion is often conveyed through eye shape and facial expressions, but Burton held firm with his design. "I used to torture [the production teams] at Disney by saying, 'It's great, there's the first character with no eyeballs.' Then they'd get all paranoid," Burton recalls. "After drawing all those foxes with their wet drippy eyes at Disney, there was a little subversion in having these characters with no eyes." It was a deliberate challenge to existing notions of how a character must look in a Disney film—or in any animated film—but in the end, Jack is just as expressive as any character with eyes. (Though it is worth noting that eyes were also optional for many of the other residents of Halloween Town, including the little corpse boy, who is magically able to cry with his eyes sewn shut.)

BELOW: Story sketch of Jack attempting to make a paper snowflake.

OPPOSITE TOP: Sketches of Jack Skellington and his trusty dog, Zero.

OPPOSITE BOTTOM: Jack Skellington dressed as Santa Claus by Tim Burton.

SALLY

For many viewers, Sally, voiced by actress Catherine O'Hara, is the heart of the film. The character went through several iterations before the filmmakers landed on her rag doll design, which draws inspiration from Mary Shelley's 1818 novel *Frankenstein*, L. Frank Baum's 1913 novel *The Patchwork Girl of Oz*, and Catwoman, one of the villains who appears in Burton's *Batman Returns*. Initially, Sally was drawn as a "sexy Bride of Frankenstein," according to Heinrichs. Burton provided her initial design, but her look in the final film shifted because of how she was characterized in the script. Originally described as a femme fatale, Sally was drawn with an hourglass figure, tight-fitting black-and-white striped dress, and ruby red lips and heels. However, when Caroline Thompson stepped in, the screenwriter wanted to ensure that Sally had the right aesthetic for the story.

"I saw the image of Sally and said, 'I can't write about that,'" she explains. "I said, 'You need to make her the Little Match Girl for me to be able to understand her.'" Thompson gave Sally a more timid persona in her script, and so the character's overall design became softer—but she still wanted her to have a degree of pluckiness. "When I saw the way they animated her, that she moved like a spider, I was inspired to strengthen her character," she says, noting that she also pulled from her own life as she created Sally. "[She] has the ability to look after herself and plots and plans and an understanding that nobody's gonna do it for her . . . That would have been me at that time."

The look of Catwoman, as played by Michelle Pfeiffer, featured a stitched-together latex costume, which inspired Sally's imagery. It was also intended as a visual reflection of her internal circumstances. "I was into stitching from the Catwoman thing, I was into that whole psychological thing of being pieced together," Burton explained of the way Sally is sewn together. "Again, these are all symbols for the way that you feel. The feeling of not being together and of being loosely stitched together and constantly trying to pull yourself together, so to speak, is just a strong feeling to me. So those kinds of visual symbols have less to do with being based on *Frankenstein* than with the feeling of pulling yourself together."

Though Sally was inspired by the more homely character of the Little Match Girl, the filmmakers also wanted her to have an undeniable allure. "I wanted to push whatever glamour the Sally puppet had to offer," explained Pete Kozachik. "We had a close-up of her just before she jumps out the window, and we studied glam photos from movies made in the 1930s and '40s and applied them to that little plastic head. Sally held her ground with the likes of Marlene Dietrich."

For Catherine O'Hara, it was a process of trial and error to discover Sally's voice. "At the beginning, I actually tried to do more of a broken voice because I thought her voice was [as] stitched up as her body," the actress remembers. "I had many recording sessions with Henry in which he directed my dialogue almost a word at a time. It didn't feel easy or organic, but it was right for Sally. She's a man-made patchwork being who's still learning how to use her body and her voice."

She adds, "I didn't know Sally would affect people the way she has. She's not quite finished and doesn't know who she is, and I guess many of us feel that way. She is in love, but until the end she believes her love might remain unrequited."

TOP: Actress Catherine O'Hara, the voice of Sally and Shock.

OPPOSITE LEFT: Early drawings of Sally from the sketchbook of Tim Burton. Sally's design was later modified to fit her more subdued personality.

OPPOSITE RIGHT TOP: Sally's puppet featured a silkscreen printed dress and thin ankles that were bolstered by her striped socks.

OPPOSITE RIGHT BOTTOM: Sally, as seen in the final film.

STOP-MO TERMS TO KNOW

SCRATCH DIALOGUE: Dialogue that is recorded early in the film's production, usually by stand-in voice actors, to be used as reference before the final voice-over is recorded.

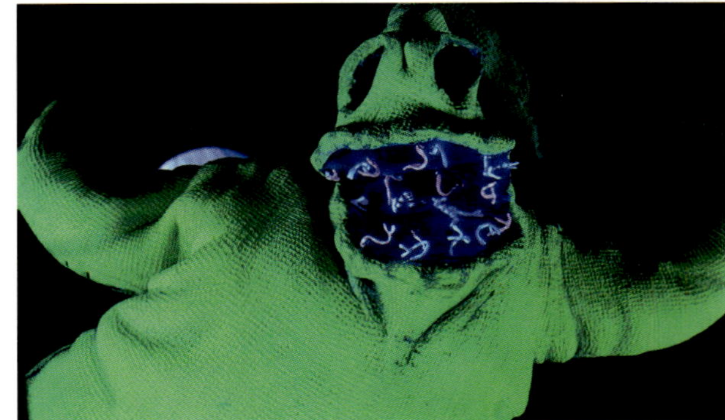

OOGIE BOOGIE

Burton may not have included the ghastly character in his original poem, but his sketch work helps Oogie Boogie clearly stand out as *Nightmare*'s primary villain—a sinister, sack-like being filled with creepy, crawly bugs. However, it took some finessing to give Oogie Boogie the right personality, and he was particularly challenging for the animators, who used a two-foot puppet to literally flesh out the stop-motion character. Although he is the antagonist, Oogie Boogie purposefully veers between overtly sinister and hilariously grotesque.

Elfman drew inspiration from Cab Calloway's bluesy song and dance numbers in the Betty Boop cartoons of the 1930s, including "Minnie the Moocher," as well as Calloway's own famous song "St. James Infirmary," for "Oogie Boogie's Song." Broadway actor Ken Page, who was enlisted to voice Oogie Boogie, similarly looked to Hollywood history to find the best speaking voice for the villain. Page ended up combining two specific influences: the Cowardly Lion in *The Wizard of Oz* (1939) and Pazuzu, the demon in *The Exorcist* (1973).

"They were going, 'Oh, okay, wow, you're as weird as we are,'" Page remembered of the filmmakers' reaction to his artistic choice. "That was where I went with it. And it's me, of course, overlaid on all of it—my ethnicity and so on. Mercedes McCambridge's work in *The Exorcist*, to me, is probably the best voice-over work of all time. A lot of what affected us psychologically was her voice. Thinking about voicing a character that was going to be animated, I wanted to try to imbue it with as much of that same depth of character, even though you weren't seeing me. I thought, 'If she could do that and scare the bejesus out of everybody, if I get anywhere near there I'm doing well.' But you didn't want to scare people completely and totally, so that was the addition of Bert Lahr [the Cowardly Lion]—lovable but still bigger than life. And, of course, I added my own hot sauce to it."

ABOVE LEFT: Early sketch of Oogie Boogie by Tim Burton.

ABOVE RIGHT TOP: Actor Ken Page, the voice of Oogie Boogie.

ABOVE RIGHT BOTTOM: Oogie Boogie, complete with glowing green skin and bug-filled insides.

EVIL SCIENTIST

Sally's on-screen inventor feels familiar and unique at the same time. The Evil Scientist, Dr. Finkelstein, is voiced by actor William Hickey and draws an obvious inspiration from Victor Frankenstein. But the wheelchair-bound character also emerged from Burton's love of a genre he calls "brain movies," such as *The Brain from Planet Arous* (1957), *The Trollenberg Terror* (1958), and *Fiend Without a Face* (1958). "He goes back to my love of any kind of horror movie and the symbols and images and types that come from any of those movies," Burton notes.

The doctor has a hunchbacked sidekick, Igor, who is part of a long line of grotesque lab assistants aiding deranged scientists on-screen, notably in the 1958 horror flick *The Revenge of Frankenstein* and Mel Brooks's *Young Frankenstein* (1974). Dr. Finkelstein controls Sally and has some villainous tendencies, but Thompson intended him to be equal parts horrible and lovable.

"Early on, I saw a drawing that someone had done—it was of a scientist in a wheelchair with his head off, scrambling his own brains," Thompson recalled. "I thought it was charming. And I wanted Sally to have an obstacle between her and Jack that was visible as opposed to emotional. So, I folded the Evil Scientist into the subplot."

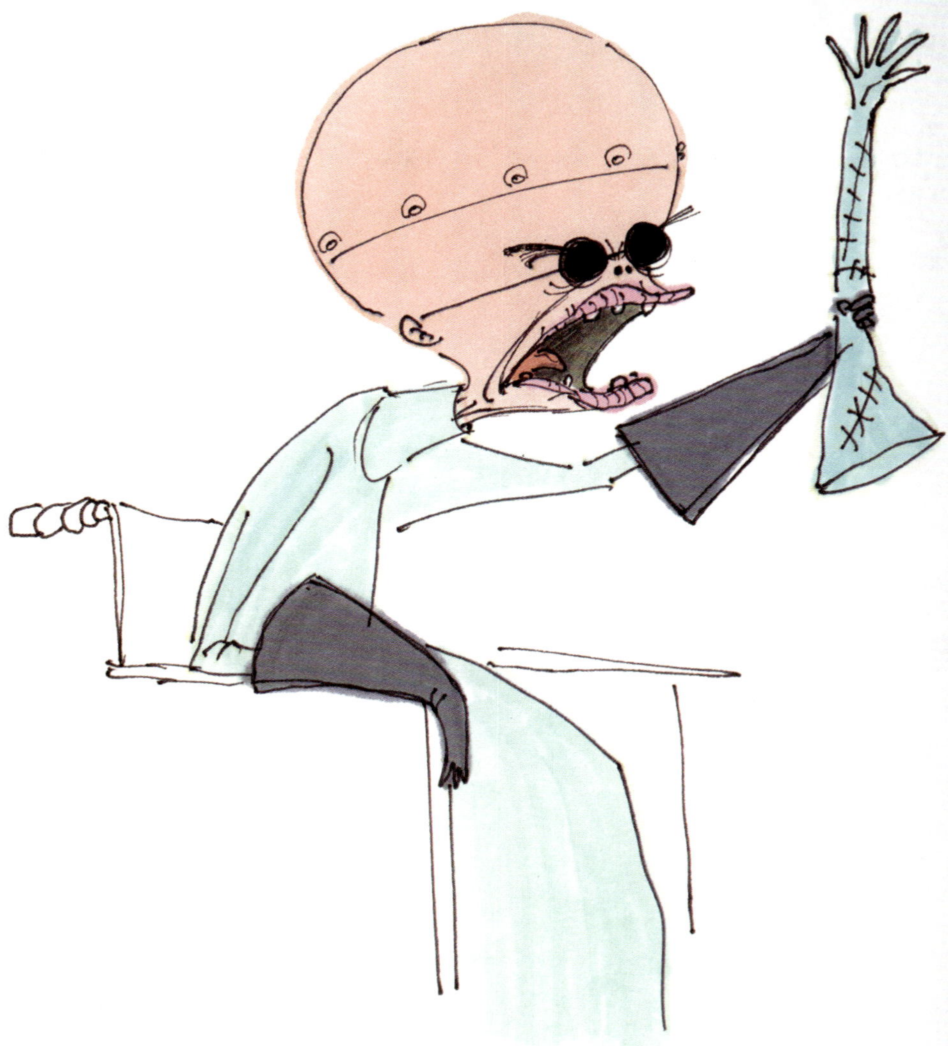

TOP: Concept art of Dr. Finkelstein, also known as the Evil Scientist.

LEFT: Dr. Finkelstein holds a skull in his laboratory where he brings the dead to life.

SANTA CLAUS

Santa Claus is a historical figure and literary character, but the incarnation in Burton's film, who is also known as "Sandy Claws," is purposefully less jolly. It was a complex interpretation, one that they eventually turned to San Francisco voice actor Ed Ivory to deliver. Other, more well-known names had originally been considered, but once Ivory recorded the scratch dialogue, Selick and Burton agreed that he was Christmas Town's perfect Santa.

"There's this juxtaposition of how Halloween is scary and Christmas is perceived as good and cheerful," the filmmaker explains. "But Santa Claus always scared me a little bit. Around Halloween you've been watching scary movies and monsters, and then Christmas comes along and you're supposed to feel happy about this big, fat guy coming down your chimney on Christmas Eve. It's like a horror movie. With Santa, I didn't want to make him a bad person—he's just kind of weird. We kept what Santa is meant to represent, but with an off-kilter quality to him."

That edginess comes through not only in Ivory's delivery but also in Santa's visual design, which retains his signature elements, like a red suit and hat, but adds an angular sensibility. "Everything was very shape-based," Heinrichs explains of designing Santa. "So, as I was doing the sculptures, Santa Claus was a huge, very fat, circular funnel shape with his head and his hat and his beard. And he had no legs. He basically was a big, round cloak that went down to the floor. You do get to see his legs, but only in a few shots. That says something about *Tim Burton's The Nightmare Before Christmas* and its handmade quality: A lot of things were specialty items that were made just for a specific shot. And in your mind that becomes a whole character, like, 'Oh, Santa has got legs.' He lives in our minds as a complete character because of those shots."

BELOW: Tim Burton's illustration of Santa Claus opening his door to the three ghoulish trick-or-treaters: Lock, Shock, and Barrel.

OPPOSITE: Concept art of Zero by Tim Burton.

ZERO

Jack Skellington's ghostly sidekick is, in typical Burton style, a trusty dog. Zero evoked several of Burton's own canine companions, as well as the character of Sparky in his short film *Frankenweenie*. The ghost pup is one of only three characters in the film who appeared in Burton's original poem, where the filmmaker described him as "the best friend that Jack had ever had."

"I had a few dogs when I was a child that were very special to me," Burton says. "They were a little heart that comes to life, so that was always something that had a power to me. It was a bond and a friendship and a feeling—a boy and his dog thing that was very important to me. I've always been lucky to have breeds that are a mixture, and I've had a couple of dogs that had an eccentricity and specialness to them."

Zero, who eventually leads Jack's sleigh, has an obvious connection with Rudolph, the reindeer who guides Santa's sleigh. The only difference is that instead of a glowing red nose, Zero has a tiny jack-o'-lantern, which appeared in Burton's original drawings of the character.

Because Zero is a ghost, his body is fluid as he floats beside Jack. He's also translucent, which was a challenge for the filmmakers, who wanted to create the character practically, rather than using computer-generated visual effects in postproduction. "Zero would always be a see-through ghost, enabling us to use simple in-camera effects," explained Kozachik. "I enjoyed the dog shots as individual puzzles to be worked out. Most shots allowed us to simply wind back the film after animating Jack and then animate Zero against a black-velvet background. We put a strong fog-effect filter on the lens anytime we filmed Zero, giving him that ghostly look."

LOCK, SHOCK, AND BARREL

Lock, Shock, and Barrel are Halloween Town's most mischievous residents. Also known as "Boogie's Boys," the trio are tasked by Jack to kidnap Santa Claus and decide to deliver him to Oogie Boogie. They appear to be young trick-or-treaters—Lock wears a devil costume, Shock is dressed as a witch, and Barrel dons a skeleton outfit—and they share a clubhouse. For Burton, the inspiration behind the trio was simple. "They are just the horrible little kids we all know or had," he says. "I have a couple—no, they're not that bad. The sort of kids we all grew up with."

The filmmaker tapped three of his regular collaborators to voice the pesky children, who have a shared musical number, "Kidnap the Sandy Claws." Both doing double duty, Elfman performed Barrel, whereas O'Hara voiced Shock. For Lock, however, Burton wanted to nod to his directorial debut. He asked Paul Reubens, who he had worked with on *Pee-wee's Big Adventure* (1985), to play Lock. The idea was to evoke Reubens' signature character while keeping the character true to the story.

"He wanted the voice to be like Pee-wee," recalled Reubens. "When you do voice work, you don't have the same tools you have as an actor; you're a voice actor, so it's really all about your voice. You have to put in as many colors and as many levels as you can. I'm proud of the work I did on it."

"I loved the experience of giving voices to Sally and Shock and I loved recording the songs," O'Hara adds. "One never really knows if their work will find an audience, but audiences just keep finding this movie."

ABOVE: Concept art of Lock, Shock, and Barrel in a snowy Halloween Town.

BELOW LEFT: Concept art of Barrel, complete with his skeleton-inspired outfit.

BELOW RIGHT: Concept art of Lock, dressed in a devilish costume.

THE MAYOR

The Mayor of Halloween Town is literally two-faced—an apt visual metaphor for how politicians say one thing and do another. The initial idea for the double visage came from a drawing by one of the artists, which Heinrichs refined through a back-and-forth with Burton. The character was voiced by Glenn Shadix, who also appeared in *Beetlejuice* as Otho. As the leader of Halloween Town, the Mayor drives a hearse, which was designed by the film's art director, Deane Taylor. It was the first sketch Taylor did when he came on board the film, and the car set the design standard for much of what came after.

"I made it ridiculously long, with tiny little wheels," Taylor says. "Which turned out to be a bit problematic because it couldn't actually drive on a lot of the roads. But that first-time rough sketch felt like the solution to all these design questions I had. I wanted to retain the spirit of that design all the way through."

LEFT: Story sketches of the Mayor climbing atop his hearse to announce the search for Jack Skellington.

BELOW: The Mayor of Halloween Town sports a black spider tie and an official orange badge, letting everyone know who's in charge.

SCULPTING THE PUPPETS

Once the beautifully unique 2D designs were in place for the sculpting team, creating 3D puppets was still no easy feat. When sketching a character who needs to move in a real environment and carry its own weight, designers had much to consider. The thickness of the legs and ankles, the size of feet, and the proportions of heads and torsos all need to be carefully considered before puppet construction begins.

When the designs are finalized, the character sketches are given as references to the sculpting team, who ultimately determines the most logical build for each character. The sculptors are masters at bringing characters to life in 3D; they are the best judges for how to realize an ink-drawn design in clay. In the case of Oogie Boogie, sculptor Norm DeCarlo knew the plan was for the character to deflate at one point, so a unique sculpture of the character was created for the sole purpose of testing that feature—though, unfortunately, that scene was cut from the film.

Every character was born from a lump of oil-based clay. The sculptor used alcohol to smooth things out and get rid of any fingerprints or smudges before the character was ready to be fired. Alcohol was used to get rid of imperfections, as opposed to water; because oil-based clay is not water soluble, it needs something harsher to break it down.

The sculpting process for Jack was much more time-consuming than any of the other characters due to his number of facial expressions. The character had around 400 unique heads that comprised his range of emotions and mouth positions for each word he spoke (see "The Head Replacement Technique," page 104). Sculptor Randal Dutra created every one of the original heads, starting from a mold made from the original Jack sculpture Rick Heinrichs created for Tim Burton in 1982. Each head made from the mold was then manually altered to create different eye and mouth positions.

OPPOSITE: Concept art of the character known as the "Harlequin Demon."

RIGHT: Puppet fabricator Lauren Vogt works on a Behemoth puppet.

Each base head shape for Jack had to be made from a mold, rather than handmade, to prevent "chatter." This stop-motion term refers to the visual error that occurs when something doesn't quite match up between frames, causing the object to appear to jump. This can happen when an object slightly changes its physical position or is replaced by a different object that doesn't quite match perfectly. For instance, if Jack's heads were switched between frames as he changed expressions but one head was slightly larger than the other, this would cause chatter. The head shape would look jumpy due to the slight change in size between frames.

Whoever created a character design, Burton reviewed each sculpture himself, either in person or through Polaroid photographs. He made notes on the Polaroids indicating what changes were needed, and then the sculptors headed back to the art department to take another pass. "There's certain physical things that slightly change the character, but for me it was always based on a feeling," Burton explains. "The puppets had to come from the spirit of what the original drawing was." This process continued until everyone was happy with the sculpt. Yet before a mold could be made from the finished sculpture, the puppet first needed bones.

TOP: Concept art of the Corpse Kid.

LEFT: Concept art for Halloween Town.

RIGHT: Concept art of the character who would later become "Behemoth." There were several iterations featuring different tools impaling his head, but ultimately an axe was chosen.

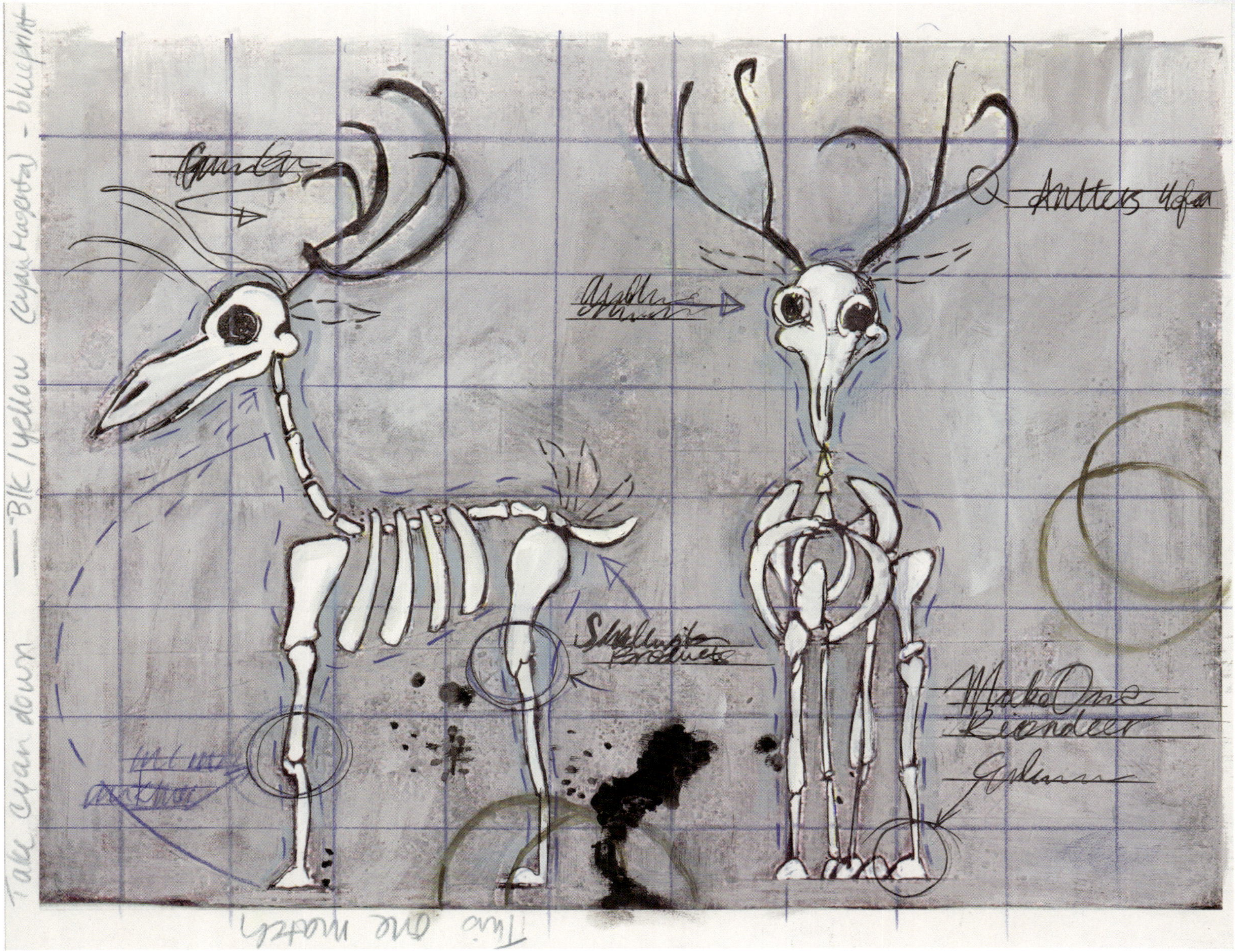

TOP: The blueprints of Dr. Finkelstein's skeletal reindeer.

RIGHT: The puppet of Zero was notoriously difficult to animate.

STOP-MO TERMS TO KNOW

CHATTER: A usually unintentional effect in stop-motion in which an object appears to move between frames. It is often a sign of amateur stop-motion, but it can sometimes be a stylistic choice.

ARMATURES

Once a character was approved by the director, armature engineers gave each puppet the gift of motion by essentially creating their skeleton—what is called an "armature." Armatures are made of metal joints that allow each puppet to move into whatever positions are necessary. The joints come in two varieties: ball joints, which give the joint an almost-universal, 360-degree range, and hinge joints, which allow for a hinge-like, open-and-closing motion. Ball joints are typically used for a body part like the neck, which needs to swivel and have a large range of motion. Hinge joints are common in hips or in the torso since the hinges can be tightened and made strong enough to hold the puppet's body weight.

To engineer the metal skeleton, the armature builders are given a front and side view drawing of each character, and if it exists, the character's finished sculpture. To speed things along, many aspects of a stop-motion production happen simultaneously, so sometimes the sculpture doesn't always come before the armature. The armature engineers determine where each of the character's joints should be. This is very important because a puppet without the proper joints could "pop"—or move positions too rapidly, making it seem less natural.

On *Tim Burton's The Nightmare Before Christmas*, the armature builders were shown the film's storyboards early on so they could visualize how each character needed to move and use the correct joints. This way, a character's actions informed the design of their armature, and the builders often acted out scenes with the armature to make sure every movement required was possible. For example, Jack as the Pumpkin King needed to be able to dance very fluidly, so the puppet's armature needed to allow for his dancer-like

BOTTOM LEFT: An armature created for one of the many puppets in *Nightmare*.

BOTTOM RIGHT: The armature for Oogie Boogie's puppet was enormous compared to the rest of the characters. It was two feet tall and weighed six pounds.

OPPOSITE: A Jack Skellington puppet alongside his armature.

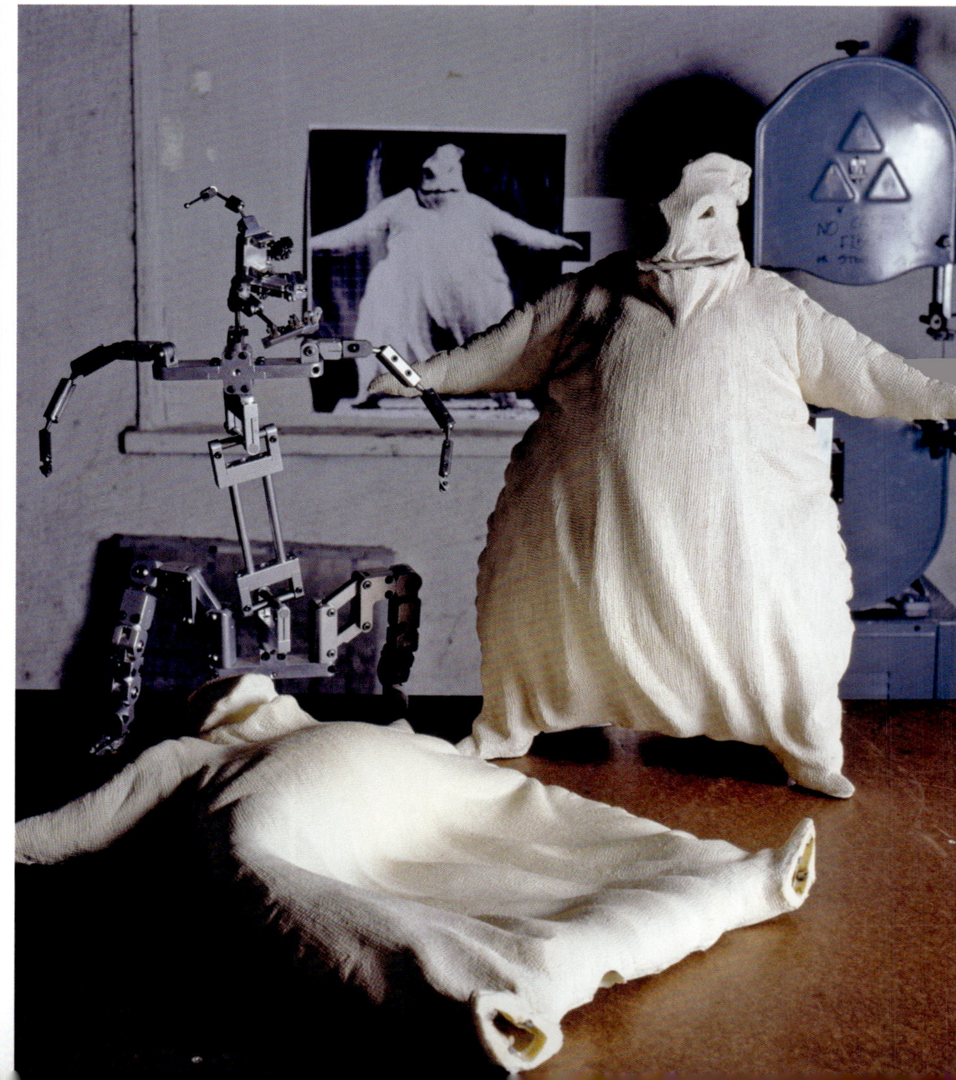

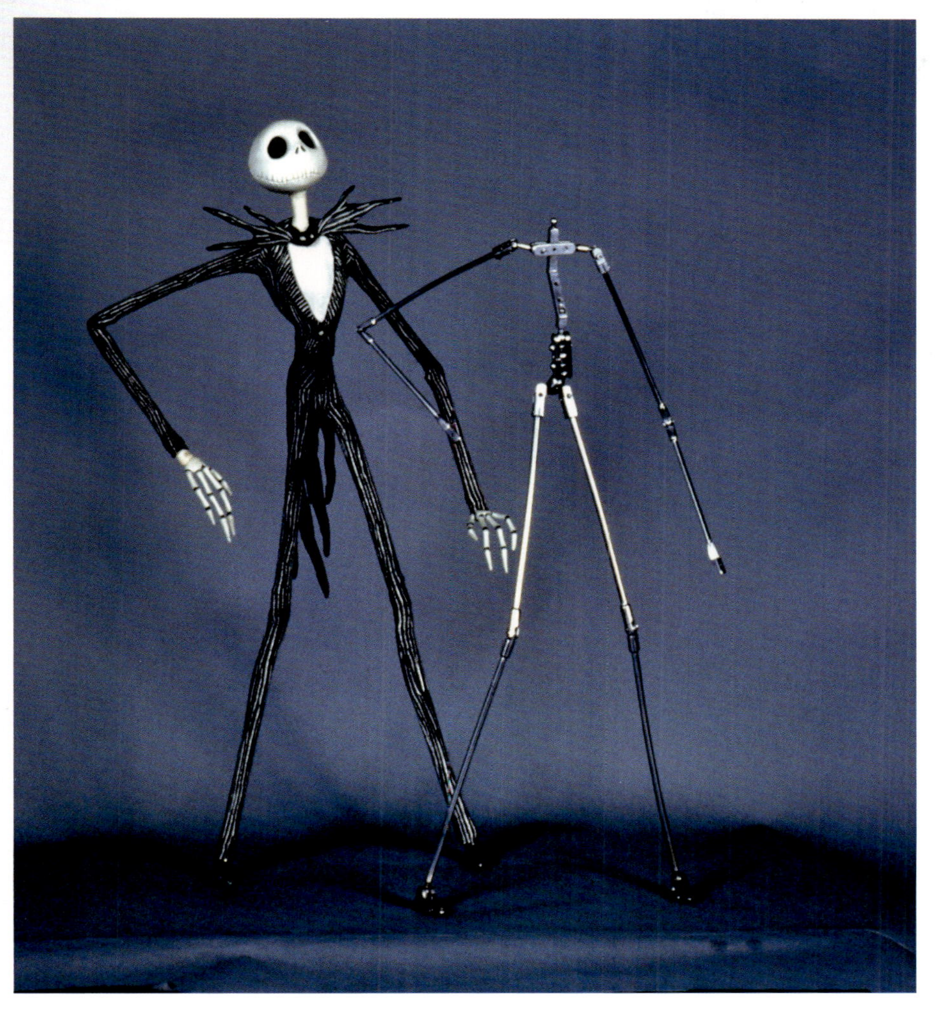

STOP-MO TERMS TO KNOW

ARMATURE: The internal skeleton of a puppet that allows it to bend at its joints. Some armatures are simply aluminum wire, whereas others are more complex, jointed skeletons made from individual metal pieces. The quality of a puppet's armature determines how smoothly an animator can bring it to life.

poses. Armature engineers typically sketch out each part of the skeleton they need to create on top of a drawing of the character. In this sketch, they make careful notes about where each joint should be located to allow the puppet to move as smoothly as possible.

A major challenge for the *Nightmare* armature team was creating armatures that followed Burton's designs but remained animator friendly. Many characters, like Jack and Sally, were drawn with thin ankles and small feet. This required careful engineering to ensure the characters could hold up the weight of their bodies. In the days before complex postproduction editing, a puppet's support rod couldn't be easily removed from every scene via visual effects. Puppets had to be sturdy enough to stand on their own. "The ankles end up being the Achilles' heel of a lot of armatures," armature engineer Chris Rand explains. The one puppet who was an exception? "The Oogie [Boogie] armature. There was no problem with that thing. [It] was so beefy, there was no snapping of ankles."

One unique puppet that broke the mold (or actually, didn't even use one!) was the creature "hiding under your bed" that appeared in the movie's introduction. The puppet didn't have any latex, cloth, or even clay—it was only a metal armature painted black with disembodied red eyes. Though an armature is usually hidden beneath layers of latex, paint, and cloth, it is probably the most important part of the puppet. "Armatures need to be practical," explains Tom St. Amand, *Nightmare*'s armature supervisor. "They are really functional things that not only have to work well, but be able to withstand a great deal of abuse and wrenching around."

Armature engineers work out their plans—including the dimensions of each individual "bone"—before they cut the metal pieces. This ensures they don't have to recut pieces, which can be wasteful and time-consuming. On *Nightmare*, the crew cut all the armatures by hand using a machine instead of any rapid-production technology. Films that need hundreds of duplicate armature pieces often use an automation program to speed the process along, but the *Nightmare* armature team was creating around only twenty duplicate parts at a time, so they stuck to hand-machined pieces. Once cut, the metal pieces were soldered with silver and received a chrome plating so they could withstand the heat of the oven without rusting. Then the armatures were ready to be placed inside the molds.

MOLDS & FABRICATION

In *Tim Burton's The Nightmare Before Christmas*, the latex puppet exteriors began with a mold made from each sculpted clay character. The clay sculpture was covered in UltraCal, a hard concrete made from gypsum rock, since a hard material works best once the mold is dry as the clay sculpture inside disintegrates into a shapeless pile of clay. Although the original sculpture is ruined, the team can now make as many copies of each character as needed—truly a bittersweet process.

A mold typically has two parts: a top and a bottom. The top usually has the character's front with the most details. The finished armature is then placed inside the mold, which is injected with liquid foam latex using a very large syringe. The foam expands around the metal armature, taking on the shape of the mold, and is then placed into a hot oven until it has cured, or hardened. The smell of baking latex is very unpleasant, like a mix of ammonia and rubber. On *Nightmare*, the Jack puppet was an exception to this process. Due to Jack's spindly shape, his puppet was mostly cast in more rigid and durable urethane, so he had a stiffer build on his body parts. Meanwhile, his joints received latex inserts to allow for extra flexibility, since he had to bend many times during animation.

When the character is peeled from the mold, the latex puppet is ready for the next stage—though sometimes errors can occur. If the puppet's armature is poking through the latex in a location that won't be covered by their clothing, it may require a complete recast of the puppet. Then the puppet goes to the fabrication department to get all the finishing touches required for its close-up.

OPPOSITE TOP: A puppet fabricator brings a Dr. Finkelstein puppet to life.

OPPOSITE BOTTOM: Some members of the puppet fabrication team.

LEFT: One of the puppet fabricators working on an Oogie Boogie Puppet.

STOP-MO TERMS TO KNOW

FLASHING AND SEAMING: Flashing refers to the buildup of material that happens along the seams of an object when it is taken out of a mold. Seaming is the delicate process of adding a thin layer of latex over the mold lines and any other imperfections caused by the molding process.

Fabrication is the final step of the puppet-making process. This team adds the fun, special details that bring each character to life, such as adding skin color, hair, and clothing. But before dressing and styling the puppets, fabricators must first clean up the imperfections made from the casting process. This includes removing the buildup of latex (called "flashing") around the character's body with tiny scissors. After it's cut, the mold lines and any other blemishes are then covered with a thin layer of liquid latex, a process called "seaming." The latex surface is then cleaned with alcohol to get it ready to be painted.

All of the foam latex puppets in *Tim Burton's The Nightmare Before Christmas* started with an airbrushed base coat of what's called "rubber cement paint." This is a liquid the crew mixed up in-house made from rubber cement, naphtha (a solvent), and a tint color. When it was first sprayed on the latex, the rubber cement paint had a popcorn effect, forming bubbles on the puppet's surface. After the surface settled back down, the rubber cement then created an elastic seal and remained very flexible.

The day-glo version of Oogie Boogie got away with just a coat of green paint, but most of the film characters, even the Wolfman, wear clothing. Surprisingly, only some of the beautiful costumes are made from actual fabric. Most of the clothing was made from painted latex, whereas others were silk-screened cloth (fabric decorated by pushing ink through a mesh screen). For instance, Sally's dress was built on top of a latex slip. It had a light gray silk screened on white cotton Lycra, and then each patchwork section was hand-painted. When light patches of Sally's dress got dirty from the natural oils in the animators' fingertips, it caused a color shift. If the fabric couldn't be cleaned properly to match the original color, the team had to strip the puppet and start again from scratch. This was one reason clothing made from painted latex was often chosen over a real piece of fabric.

Jack's iconic pinstripe suit was made by a freelance seamstress. This was mainly because sewing a miniature suit was a difficult and time-consuming task for a crew that was building dozens of puppets at the same time. Since Jack's body was cast with hard urethane instead of foam, his suit had nothing to cling to, which resulted in "chatter," as the pinstripes moved between frames and seemed to be jumping around during animation. To fix this, the fabrication department added adhesive under Jack's suit—just enough to make the fabric stick better without visibly bleeding through the fabric. "The best creativity comes to fruition in those kinds of circumstances," says Bonita DeCarlo, the character fabric supervisor.

These fixes occurred so often in the fabrication department that a "puppet hospital" was created. When a puppet's latex got too worn or a fabric too dirty, the fabrication team came to the rescue and either repaired the puppet or stripped it down and started from scratch. At some point, every puppet, possibly with the exception of Santa's elves, needed to have its latex cut from the armature and fully rebuilt from the casting stage. The work of the fabricators was truly never done, and the puppet-building process continued up until the very end of production.

TOP: The "puppet hospital," used for the maintenance of the various puppets during production. The fabrication department of Skellington Productions was the home for all puppets—in any form—including all the materials used to create them.

OPPOSITE: The center of Halloween Town, filled with its residents.

CHAPTER 5

BUILDING WORLDS, CREATING MAGIC

"You go home with backaches, you cut yourself on wire, but you do get into this Zen mode—this funky groove. When you have brought something to life, it is really rewarding."

—TRAVIS KNIGHT, PRESIDENT AND CEO OF LAIKA

Creating a convincing world for any film is no easy feat. In a live-action film, location scouts are tasked with the herculean effort of finding the perfect environments for each scene, ensuring the sites are authentic, visually appealing, and practical for all involved. In the world of stop-motion, however, every location dreamed up by the director and art department must be created from scratch. Each light source needs to be carefully considered for each scene, and set dressers act as interior decorators, curating each piece of furniture, each floor or wallpaper pattern, and each unique prop found in every set.

In *Tim Burton's The Nightmare Before Christmas*, the characters weren't limited to the puppets alone—the environments they populated also became integral players in the story. Even more fascinating is that *Nightmare*'s actual filming location technically never changed. Skellington Productions, the old, hallowed warehouse, needed to hold the film's entire miniature world, including Halloween Town, Christmas Town, and the Real World.

SET DESIGN

PAGE 80: Concept art of Halloween Town Square.

OPPOSITE: Early concept art of Halloween Town, designed by Tim Burton.

BELOW: Concept art of Oogie Boogie in his lair by assistant art director Kelly Asbury.

The very first set built for *Tim Burton's The Nightmare Before Christmas* was Christmas Town, a location inspired by famed children's book author Dr. Seuss. Assistant art director Kendal Cronkhite, who was responsible for the design of Christmas Town, wanted the landscape to be "soft and sloppy." With its rolling lines and vibrant lights, the set also needed to act as an apt juxtaposition with Jack Skellington's hometown. "It's Dr. Seuss and bright colors, like candy," she explained.

The Halloween Town set was perhaps the most "Burtonesque" of all the *Nightmare* locations. It's dark and gothic, with an off-kilter balance and dangerous, sharp angles, and was inspired by the visual style of the 1920 German silent horror film *The Cabinet of Dr. Caligari*. Assistant art director Kelly Asbury claimed Henry Selick's guidance on creating the frightening world was "to be something that, if you ran your hand over it, it would cut you." The palate was mostly monochrome, with a few small accents of orange and green. Black buildings were given white accents to create an etched effect, like a drawing. The mood of Halloween Town was intended to capture the feeling of Burton's sketches and to show clear inspiration from old horror movies without coming off as cliché. The gothic, pen-and-ink drawings of American illustrator Edward Gorey were also a big influence on the town's design.

ABOVE: Art director Kelly Asbury's depiction of a structure in Halloween Town.

OPPOSITE TOP: A sketch of Jack's staircase and gate by assistant art director Kendal Cronkhite.

OPPOSITE CENTER: Concept art of Dr. Finkelstein's lab by assistant art director Kelly Asbury.

OPPOSITE BOTTOM: Concept art of Halloween Town, created by art director Kelly Asbury.

Art director Deane Taylor recalls, "Halloween Town needed to be gothic and have a sense of humor." This humor shows up in all the wonderful little details like the hanging spider doorbell that screams to announce visitors to Jack's house, the Mayor's car siren powered by cranking the tail of a yowling metal cat, and the head peeking from inside the musician's bass that some say resembles composer Danny Elfman. Taylor adds that other artistic choices for the town were given a deeper storyline, like the color of all the water sources. "The backstory was that there is a toxic green, poisonous underground river. So wherever there's a drain or a manhole cover that's off, the green light will shine up through it," he explains. "That gave us the chance to either warm up a shot or cool it down but still stay within the range of black, white, and orange."

Jack's house, arguably the most famous home in Halloween Town, defies the known laws of physics. Taylor inverted the towering structure, which sits atop an unsupported set of steps, purposefully making it "upside down and sort of strange." Its gaunt lines and unusual design evoke Jack himself, and the designers weren't concerned with realism in its design. According to set builder Todd Lookinland, "The way we were building it, we could make these fanciful things that wouldn't work in the real world. That stuff was a lot of fun to build."

The crew had as much fun with Dr. Finkelstein's laboratory, which has the appearance of a water tower but somewhat literally shows that a lot of *thinking* went into its exterior design. "The shape of Dr. Finkelstein's head is the shape of his laboratory, which is like a cartoon of his big head," says visual consultant Rick Heinrichs. "Everything has a certain meaning and a connection to the character that it's associated with—the Mayor to his car, Jack to his house, Sally and her room and how she escapes the room, and the environs of Halloween Town. All those things are, as they always are in animation, very character-based."

Designing the film's Real World, in contrast, required an aesthetic that set it far apart from Halloween Town and Christmas Town. It needed to be less fantastical but still unique. Or as Taylor puts it: "We wanted to make it look like the least interesting part of the world [of the film]."

To achieve this, the Real World and its characters were given a rigid and flat feeling, very unlike the more dynamic and fluid characters in both Halloween Town and Christmas Town. The art department completed the sketches of the Real World using 3D drawing paper, which is an isometric drawing pad featuring a grid entirely made of sixty-degree triangles. Though not a typical requirement of designing for a stop-motion film, it allowed the drawings to be three-dimensional but in isometric perspective—which has the opposite effect of a fish-eye lens and makes things appear less distorted. The parallel lines within this perspective created a juxtaposition to the more exaggerated perspective found in the film's other worlds.

Once the art department finished their concept illustrations, the set design team took over. Even though they all did amazing work, it was the first time any of the team's artists had worked on designs in 3D space. "My first task was to pop out the drawings," remembers set designer and dressing supervisor Gregg Olsson. "To literally think, okay, how big does this have to be to function for a camera lens, animator access . . . Is it going to fit on a stage? How do we break it apart?" Olsson and his team were tasked with creating a quarter-scale mock-up of each set. Because these were just initial mock-ups to test out the sets, they were detailed but not sturdy, as they were often made of cardboard or plywood and put together with hot glue.

These set models acted as guidelines for the set construction team, outlining everything from textures and paint to how the actual set would break apart. Director Henry Selick used the models, along with a viewfinder (an unattached camera lens), to plan out how each shot would look on set. After the set team knew the angles of the proposed shots, they could plan where the set needed to break apart to allow for the animators and the camera people to do their magic.

The amount of work put into creating just the set models is a true testament to a stop-motion crew's level of dedication. In a high-quality film like *Tim Burton's The Nightmare Before Christmas*, the stop-motion sets are considered an art form themselves. During *Nightmare*'s production, the set models were so integral to creating the finished set pieces that members of the art department often painted the models and made sure colors and textures were accurate before passing off the finished products to the construction team. The goal was to make the models clear enough for the set construction team so the art department's preferences were carried over to the final set while allowing the set-building process to remain somewhat organic.

RIGHT: Concept art of elf houses in Christmas Town by assistant art director Kendal Cronkhite.

FARTHER RIGHT: Santa's shadow on the snow in Christmas Town created by storyboard supervisor Joe Ranft.

BOTTOM: Art of Timmy's bedroom in the Real World, created by assistant art director Kendal Cronkhite.

OPPOSITE TOP: Concept art of Santa's workshop, featuring elves hard at work making candy canes.

OPPOSITE BOTTOM: Concept art of the Christmas Town train by assistant art director Kendal Cronkhite.

SET CONSTRUCTION

A major consideration when building sets for stop-motion is accommodating the animators, who must be able to move freely around the set to adjust the puppets. Most animators prefer not to reach over two feet to adjust a puppet, as it can get strenuous when animating for hours at a time, plus there is more potential to disrupt the set. Segmented set pieces that can be broken apart are necessary to prevent animators from having to climb on sets and damage the impressive work of the set construction team. If a set can't be broken apart in less than two-foot sections, trap doors are usually added to the set floor so an animator can pop up and adjust the puppet before each frame. Because some *Nightmare* sets were very large, sectioning them allowed to more easily transport the set to the stage, and it allowed the camera to be repositioned to achieve different camera angles. "Trying to get a set that was reasonably comfortable for an animator to stand and work at for twelve, fourteen hours a day was a huge task that we were given," set construction supervisor Lee "Bo" Henry says.

The *Nightmare* set construction team created, on average, two and a half sets per week. By the end of production, the team had created around 215 total sets. Some sets, like the Town Hall, had duplicates. That way, filming could take place on one set while dressing and prep happened on another. The Halloween Town exterior set had four versions—each with the same number of cobblestones perfectly mirrored to protect continuity. Skellington Productions had about eighteen stages that featured sets of all sizes: some were greater than twenty feet in diameter, and others were just one square foot, depending on how many puppets or other objects were present in the scene.

TOP: The final scene of Jack and Sally on a snow-covered Spiral Hill.

OPPOSITE TOP: Animation supervisor Eric Leighton tests the gigantic Oogie Boogie puppet on the roulette wheel set.

OPPOSITE BOTTOM: Oogie Boogie in his lair.

Sometimes entire sets were built for a scene that lasts mere seconds on screen, like Jack's reflection in the doorknob as he opens the door to Christmas Town. That shot required a new set as well as a tube large enough for the animator, Mike Belzer, to crawl in and out of while animating the Jack puppet. Showing the actual reflection in the doorknob required the tube to cover what would normally be picked up by the camera lens, and it was replaced by a hand-painted reflection of the surrounding Hinterlands, the mysterious in-between land with seven holiday-themed trees (Christmas, Halloween, Valentine's Day, Easter, St. Patrick's Day, Independence Day, and Thanksgiving) that act as a gateway to and from Halloween Town. Art director Deane Taylor painted what the vision of the forest would be, and the camera lens was carefully hidden within a blurry tree in the background. The reflection was painted to create a forced perspective, or the illusion that what's seen was farther away than it really was. Taylor also remembers how transforming the magical Hinterland trees into a viable set proved equally challenging. "I think they stood about three meters tall," he says. "They had to be big enough for Jack, who was quite tall, to fall into comfortably."

Perhaps Jack wouldn't have fallen into the Christmas Town tree if he was with Bo Henry (later the art director on *Coraline*, 2009), who was known for creating extremely sturdy sets that were cross-braced and heavily reinforced. This was necessary not only to prevent the need to rebuild sets but also to protect an animator's shot. If a set wasn't sturdy enough to keep buildings and props from toppling over, weeks of work could be ruined from a shaky foundation. "We would make jokes about the way Bo built sets," animator Angie Glocka recalls. "They were built like a truck could drive on them." This stability allowed for the continual wear and tear created by animators and camera people, but the sets could also be a nightmare for set dressers attempting to climb under the structures to wire lights. In the scene where Jack marvels at Christmas Town, all of the lights on the houses below were lit with fiber optics, which had threads that needed to be snaked and bundled beneath the intricate set to hide the wires. "I had to weave myself through his structure . . . through all the cross-bracing," says set dresser Gretchen Scharfenberg, who also jokes. "I always said the best place to be in an earthquake would be underneath one of [Bo Henry's] sets."

STOP-MO TERMS TO KNOW

FORCED PERSPECTIVE: A technique that uses optical illusion to make something seem either closer, farther away, smaller, or larger than it really is.

Among the most recognizable locations in *Tim Burton's The Nightmare Before Christmas* is the mysterious Spiral Hill, located just beyond the graveyard in Halloween Town. Jack retreats to the hill while he achingly wishes for something more than endless scares. The Spiral Hill in that scene, which features the song "Jack's Lament," was actually a combination of a puppet and a set piece. Constructed by model maker Marc Ribaud, the hill contained its own armature (an internal poseable skeleton) that unfurled a long, uncurling branch at the same time Jack retreated downhill. Jack's tiny feet were attached to the structure using a screw and washer through a hole in his foot (known as a tie down), and animator Tim Hittle had to carefully animate the spindly hill branch at the same time he animated the puppet, so that the puppet hit his marks. "It was constantly unraveling, he was constantly stepping, and there were a lot of times I thought, 'Oh, he's gonna miss it!'" Hittle remembers. But the beauty of the set paired with the expert animation was a huge success, making this one of the most memorable and iconic shots of the film.

The actual structure of the set was, of course, incredibly important to the look of the film, and the scenic department added the magic of the hand-painted details. "We would build these sets that were made out of wood, for the most part, and then hand them over to the scenic department," Todd Lookinland reflects. "And then they would be completely transformed into these incredible works of art."

After the structure of the set was finished, clay or plaster was often spread over top, and lines were carved into it to create texture and give it that signature illustrated look that the art department desired. Each finished set was a joint effort between the set construction and scenic teams to make sure it was structurally sound and visually accurate to the original designs.

Along with the many dazzling foreground details of each set, the skies of Halloween Town and Christmas Town were certainly critical. Artist B.J. Fredrickson painted huge backdrops of sky with a spray gun, and each world features a different style: Halloween Town has ominous black, white, and gray clouds that Frederickson describes as reminiscent of the classic *Frankenstein* films. Notably, Christmas Town features the film's only illuminated night sky. "Jack's first view of Christmas Town includes the only stars in the movie," said Pete Kozachik. "We built a dozen or two: a black card with cutout pointy stars taped to clamp lights. Pressed from behind a blue muslin backing was a night sky with movable stars." This made the Christmas Town skies suitably more realistic and colorful than those of Halloween Town.

LEFT: Dr. Finkelstein bringing some of his creations to life.

OPPOSITE TOP: Set builders Phil Brotherton (left) and Todd Lookinland (right) in front of the famous Spiral Hill set.

OPPOSITE BOTTOM: A model of one of the houses that Santa Jack visits in the Real World.

LIGHTING

Once *Nightmare*'s beautifully intricate sets were built, the team gave them light. German expressionism, just one of several inspirations for the film, has two key features: harsh shadows and dramatic lighting. This was a normal request for a Tim Burton film, as he leans toward a dark, gothic aesthetic with high contrast. But in the world of stop-motion, lighting is typically high-key (bright, with little contrast) and soft. Stop-motion films are usually lit quite brightly to clearly show the animation without losing it in the puppet's shadow. "As stop-motion animators, we're always overlighting things a little," Henry Selick explains, "so it was scary to go where Tim [Burton] wanted us."

Though the film was shot in full color, the lighting technicians used similar techniques as those used in black-and-white cinematography. This was due to the film's mainly black-and-white color scheme, as well as the strong influence of early twentieth-century German expressionist cinema. The sets were lit similarly to a live-action film, though the light sources were much smaller.

A great amount of planning goes into lighting a stop-motion set. "In live action, you can hide a light behind a column or place it overhead," Bo Henry explains. "Here, a light is bigger than the entire set, so we have to plan on that from the beginning."

Tim Burton's The Nightmare Before Christmas used two basic types of lighting: traditional, overhead movie-set lights, which are out of view of the audience, to illuminate the overall scene, and practical lights from sources that are physically in the scene and help build the world on screen. These practical lights included lanterns, Zero's pumpkin nose, car lights, and Christmas lights. White paint was often added to parts of buildings that needed more of a reflection effect when practical lights couldn't be added.

Some scenes required twenty to thirty various light sources, and the most common light was the two-hundred-watt mini. This bulb was great for

BELOW: Homes in the Real World were lit by practical lights, like Timmy's green floor lamp seen here.

OPPOSITE TOP: The train that travels through Christmas Town, which is very reminiscent of the concept art.

OPPOSITE CENTER: Santa's shadow on the snow in Christmas Town, as seen in the final film.

OPPOSITE BOTTOM: An aerial view of Christmas Town.

selective lighting but horrible for longevity. They burn out frequently, which posed a major issue for animators. They could become so consumed with their shot that they didn't notice when a bulb burned out—and this was often discovered only later in dailies when the shot was seen on the big screen. Luckily, the animation was usually salvageable, but if the lighting change was too obvious, it required a reshoot.

One way to account for a bulb burnout was using a method known as a "second pass." The film was wound back to the first frame of the shot and then filmed again with the entire set dark except for the one light that burned out. The one lit area would then be double exposed onto the existing film to essentially create a new layer. This is not an easy technique, and it was often not worth the risk of ruining the shot completely. Instead, a team at Skellington Productions created a light alarm that alerted the crew when the voltage being used on the set dropped below a specific threshold. This new technology, invented just for this film, was another way *Nightmare* was a trailblazer in large-scale stop-motion productions.

STOP-MO TERMS TO KNOW

DOUBLE EXPOSURE: When a frame of film is exposed to light twice (or multiple times) to create additional layers of an image on the frame. The technique was used to add special effects to *Nightmare* in a time before heavy postproduction editing was possible.

SET DRESSING & PROPS

Set, lights . . . action? Not yet. Before rolling the cameras, set dressers needed to fill in all the little details that made the world of *Nightmare* come to life. Set dressers are responsible for everything from adding practical lights to securing all the hand-crafted props within each environment. These props are built by the model-making crew, and they include any decorations from floor to ceiling. In the Real World, the home interiors feature a wealth of realistic details, like the plates on the wall of little Timmy's house featuring an Elvis-like character. These "blink and you'll miss them" elements make the homes feel lived-in and the characters more human and relatable.

Thousands of props were needed for the sets of *Nightmare*. Some were as small as an inch long, like many of the toys created for the "Making Christmas" scene. Yet the details needed to be strong enough for close-ups, too. Props were created from several different materials—from plywood and epoxy putty to aluminum foil-covered paper and so much more. Foil was a popular choice for props that required the appearance of paper but needed to be pliable for animation. If you look at Santa Jack's list of children or the Mayor's speech, which he reads before Jack's takeoff, they are sheets of paper with foil sandwiched between them to allow them to wave like a real sheet of

BELOW: Concept art of Christmas Town by assistant art director Kendal Cronkhite.

OPPOSITE: Dr. Finkelstein's tower, which derives its shape from its resident's head.

paper. Occasionally, molds were made for props that needed multiples, like the pies featured in Christmas Town.

Some of the most complex set pieces and props are in Oogie Boogie's Lair, which was one of a few sets that didn't start with original sketches from Tim Burton. Deane Taylor describes the set piece as a dungeon with casino décor, and it took several months of sketching to land on the final design. The art department drew inspiration from casinos and cave paintings, and director Henry Selick came up with the idea to use UV paint and black lights to decorate the cavernous lair. The use of darkness and light created two entirely different vibes and added to the eerie feeling of Oogie Boogie's menacing playground. The set also included six duplicates of a completely functional roulette wheel made from a simple motor and bicycle chain, as well as real working lights that were installed around the edge of the wheel. "The spinning casino wheel lights up, and it's got hearts and clubs and diamonds and spades, as well as skeleton heads," remembers Todd Lookinland. "That set was so fun to build because it had this whole mechanical aspect to spin. . . . but it was difficult to build that."

Each new set and prop was so fun and exciting to build that many of the set builders and model makers recall fighting over which pieces they got to create. Every detail of the magical world of *Nightmare* was crafted with such thought, care, and passion by the dedicated set artists. Their commitment to the film and to the art of stop-motion clearly shows in the finished film and is a major reason it has stood up as a classic over all these years.

CHAPTER 6

ANIMATING A STOP-MOTION MUSICAL

"As an animator, you are a god—you make the world, populate it, and bring it to life."

—PETER LORD, COFOUNDER OF AARDMAN ANIMATIONS

When Tim Burton decided that his poem "The Nightmare Before Christmas" should be presented as a stop-motion film, a whole world of possibilities opened up. Jack wasn't just a spindly skeleton in pinstripes anymore. In the film, he is an elegant dancer with a wonderfully expressive face and a gift for reciting poignant prose. The Mayor swivels his face around and Dr. Finkelstein scratches his brain (really, his actual brain), among a host of other unique and captivating personality quirks. All of this is thanks to the people who brought this world to life—the tireless animation crew.

THE BASICS OF STOP-MOTION ANIMATION

PAGE 96: Jack Skellington in front of the gates to his house.

BELOW: Jack Skellington in the Hinterlands.

OPPOSITE TOP: Oogie Boogie's shadow on the moon at night.

OPPOSITE BOTTOM: The three musicians from *Tim Burton's The Nightmare Before Christmas.*

The idea of animation as a performance is truly exemplified in stop-motion. If the armature is the puppet's skeleton, the animator is the puppet's heart—pumping the metaphorical lifeblood into an otherwise lifeless figure. The puppet takes action in a real location, with real sets, props, lighting, and a camera crew. "There's such an energy about it. Seeing real sets, lights . . . it's like being a giant in a movie studio," Burton says. One of the only things that sets stop-motion apart from a live-action film is that the actors are transferring their carefully planned performance to an articulated puppet. Each movement required of the puppet is premeditated and calculated to work within the confines of time and space.

Because all the puppets must stand on their own to get the perfect shot, they require what are called tie downs, which essentially keep the puppet in place anywhere on the set. The process of creating tie downs starts with one person drilling a hole from underneath the set and another person fastening it to the puppet's feet with a screw and washer. By the end of a shot, a set could be completely riddled in tie down holes, based on how much the puppet moves around its environment. The animator is tasked with plugging up the holes, usually with clay, to cover up any that may be visible in the current shot.

In *Tim Burton's The Nightmare Before Christmas*, the animation was shot "on ones," meaning twenty-four frames of film were shot per second of movie time. For example, when Jack knocks over his house of playing cards, one second of the finished scene is actually made up of twenty-four

STOP-MO TERMS TO KNOW

TIE DOWN: Refers to either the mechanism or the method of securing a puppet to a set. A tie down is a small metal connector, usually a screw, that is embedded into the puppet's feet and screwed down into a hole in the set and fastened with a washer.

ON ONES: This term refers to shooting twenty-four frames per second of film, in which every frame is a unique image. Shooting "on twos" refers to animating twelve frames per second, or repeating each image for two frames (to add up to twenty-four frames per second). Similarly, "on threes "means shooting eight frames per second, so each image appears for three frames.

individual frames. The animator, in this case Angie Glocka, repositioned the cards for each of those twenty-four frames. Once those frames are strung together, it creates the illusion of movement, and the cards fall to the table in a realistic flow.

The concept sounds simple on paper, but due to the tedious process of repositioning puppets and objects for each frame, stop-motion animation is a grueling endeavor. Due to its complexity, the entire shot of Jack walking around in his tower and knocking over the house of cards took Angie Glocka around ten days to complete. Many shots that show the effects of gravity, like the Mayor tumbling down the stairs or Santa Jack flying out of his sleigh, required extra help to keep the puppets in position. The animators became very familiar with fishing line, sticky wax, and sometimes actual rigs to hold the puppet either stationary or suspended in air.

Complex shots might be nearly impossible to get right without the help of a frame grabber, a tool that lets animators view the current frame they are working on as well as toggle back to the two previous frames. This tool helps assess how

TOP: Jack with his house of Christmas cards in a scene animated by Angie Glocka.

OPPOSITE TOP: A frame of Jack in one of many musical numbers.

OPPOSITE BOTTOM: Jack's reflection appears in the doorknob to Christmas Town. Though a seemingly simple shot, it actually required clever planning.

the shot is progressing, and it is especially helpful if something goes wrong. Occasionally, a puppet must be moved back to its previous position and reshot, which is called a "cut back." A burned-out light on set, a puppet that requires mending, or any general disruption to shooting can warrant a cut back. The animator then needs to hold up a sign in front of the camera that reads "cut back one frame" and take a photo, for the film editor to adjust accordingly. Going back a frame also requires rewinding the motion-controlled camera rig, which requires calling in the camera operator for assistance. Clearly, messing up a frame is something animators try to avoid.

Prior to having a frame grabber, animators tracked the progress of their animation using a tool called a surface gauge, which is essentially a solid, heavy base with a long vertical pole sticking out of it. The tip of the pole is adjustable, so it can be set up to point at a specific part of the puppet when animation begins, and it stays in that position while the puppet is adjusted. As movement progresses, the surface gauge keeps the original place, so animators can see how far the puppet has moved since the beginning of the shot. Although frame grabbers were used on *Nightmare*, many animators still used surface gauges as another way to track their progress.

STOP-MO TERMS TO KNOW

RIG: A support structure that holds and stabilizes characters or objects during the filming process.

FRAME GRABBER: A tool that allows animators to see their current frame and two previous frames on a screen in to check the progress of their shot.

CUT BACK: The act of moving the puppet back into its most recent position and reshooting the very last frame.

SURFACE GAUGE: A stop-motion tool that allows the animator to place an adjustable arm at a specific point in space in order to track how far they've moved the object they're animating.

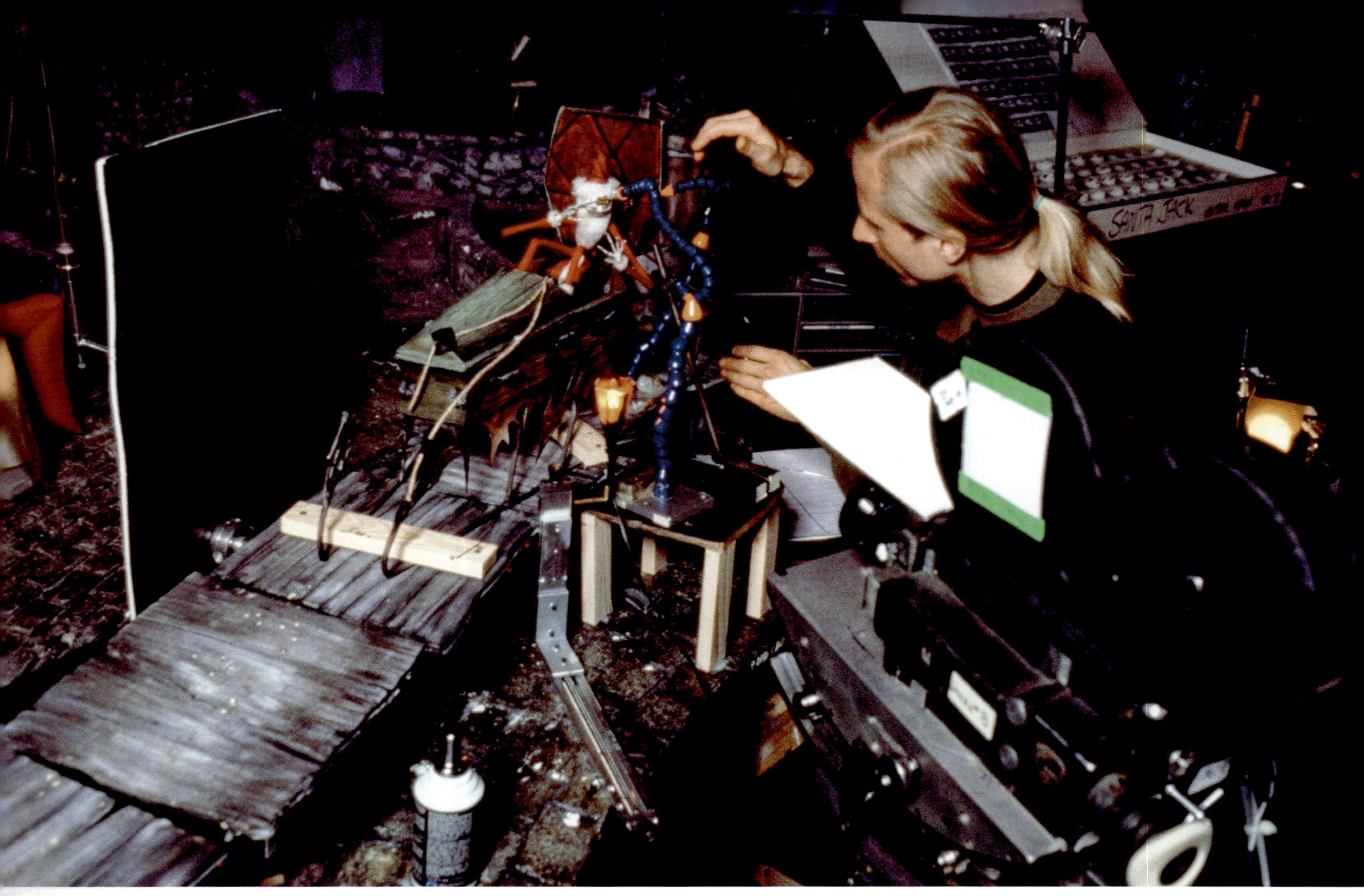

ASSIGNING THE SHOTS

Though some shots in the film, like Jack's tumbling house of cards, were inherently more difficult than others, shot assignments were typically at the discretion of animation supervisor Eric Leighton or director Henry Selick. Shots were often assigned based on what storyboard was complete, which set was built, or which puppet was ready for its close-up. Because the many stages of production were often happening simultaneously, the animation crew had to wait until scenes made it to their stop on the production pipeline.

Shots were also sometimes assigned based on an animator's strong suit or their particular animation style. Some animators had a knack for working with certain puppets, like animators Trey Thomas and Tim Hittle, who excelled at giving life to Sally despite her puppet being unforgiving at times. "She had more emotional depth than the other characters in the film," Hittle recalls. "I tried to show that with my shots . . . I think less was more with her." Fellow animator Mike Belzer and director of photography Pete Kozachik both attributed Hittle's success with Sally to a newly budding relationship he was involved with during production. Perhaps the intimate scenes between Jack and Sally on Spiral Hill needed an animator inspired by their own romantic feelings. So much of an animator's frame of mind can easily be transferred to the puppet they're animating.

Though most assignments were out of the animators' hands, the crew could lobby for a shot if it was available. Animator Owen Klatte loved Oogie Boogie's Cab Calloway–esque song. Even with the challenge of animating a two-foot-tall puppet, Klatte asked to be assigned to the jazzy dance number, and Leighton and Selick kindly agreed. Similarly, animator Anthony Scott asked to be assigned the entire weighty graveyard scene

TOP: Animator Joel Fletcher working with Jack in his Santa costume.

during the musical number "Poor Jack." "The first time I read the script, I immediately connected to that sequence. It was all about transformation, Jack realizing who he is and embracing it," Scott remembers. "I asked Eric and Henry if I could animate it and was extremely fortunate to have been given it."

Animators were usually assigned an entire sequence on the same set, which could run anywhere from five to fifteen shots in a row, making them easier to edit together. Keeping the same animator for consecutive shots, rather than splitting consecutive shots among several animators, usually made switching animators less obvious, but that wasn't always possible. Though it might not be obvious to the audience, *Nightmare* animators could often identify which animator did which shot, based on their style. However, leaving one's trademark in a shot isn't considered a good thing. "Part of being a good animator is being able to animate a character in a way that fits seamlessly with how other animators have animated it so that the performance, the personality of the character, is consistent no matter who has animated it," Owen Klatte explains.

OPPOSITE: Tommy Tune as Ambrose Kemper in *Hello, Dolly!* (1969). Tune was used as animation reference for Jack Skellington due to his height.

BELOW: Trey Thomas animating part of the "Making Christmas" sequence.

To keep that consistency, animation supervisor Eric Leighton spent his early days on *Nightmare* perfecting Jack's graceful walking style in order to provide a reference for the animators joining his crew. The animators got inspired by watching videos of dancers Fred Astaire (*Holiday Inn*, 1942), Gene Kelly (*Singin' in the Rain*, 1952), and Tommy Tune (*Hello Dolly!*, 1969)—the latter, due to his six-foot-seven frame, served as the perfect model for Jack's gangly figure. The reference material ensured each animator was bringing the same version of Jack to life in each scene, whether walking proudly through Halloween Town or waltzing through the snow-covered world of Christmas Town.

Old tapes of famous dancers helped establish Jack's general demeanor, but for each individual shot with a new set of unique actions, the animators relied on storyboards, recordings of the songs and dialogue, and even the acting chops of Henry Selick himself. Before any shot was approved for a "pop-through"—in which an animator shows roughly every fifth frame of a sequence to receive feedback—and ultimately given the go-ahead to "launch the shot," as the crew called it, Selick would meet with an animator to have their shot explained, and often acted out, to make sure everything turned out as closely as possible to how the director envisioned it. "As an animator, you have to get used to looking silly," Klatte says. "You have to act out all these goofy things that the characters are going to do."

STOP-MO TERMS TO KNOW

POP-THROUGH: A very basic run-through of the major poses in a shot in which the animator typically shows every fifth frame (or less) of a sequence to get the director's feedback before shooting the final animation.

THE HEAD REPLACEMENT TECHNIQUE

Another tool that brought the Jack puppet to life was the head replacement technique. Jack's head was swapped out for each frame of animation, so every time the animator moved the puppet, Jack received a new facial expression based on his mood and the syllable of the word he was speaking. Concept artist Jorgen Klubien drew every possible facial expression needed for all of Jack's scenes throughout the film, and the sculpting team created almost four hundred variants of Jack's face. In Sally's case, only a replacement face was required so as not to disrupt her hair.

The technique required extensive planning. Before shooting, track reader Dan Mason arranged computer images of each replacement head to be used in the proper order, then he played the images at twenty-four frames per second to visualize how the puppet's face would look in the final animation. This was adjusted until it was perfect, and each frame was assigned a head. These plans were then given to the animator so they knew which head to swap in with each frame.

Each animator had their own pack of replacement heads that they kept with them on set. Sometimes specialty heads were required for a particular shot, like Jack's scream face, that weren't included in the standard pack of heads. Finally, puppets that didn't use the replacement head technique had facial features that could be altered mechanically by the animator. The shape of mouths or the position of eyebrows could be manually changed via wires and paddles built into the puppet's face.

DAILIES: THE ANIMATOR'S JUDGMENT DAY

Every animator has their own personal feelings about dailies, the film industry term for reviewing and taking notes on new footage with an audience of crew members. In the case of *Tim Burton's The Nightmare Before Christmas*, this included both newly animated test shots and final shots that needed Henry Selick's approval. It was simultaneously the most exciting and most stressful period of the day at Skellington Productions, and it happened first thing in the morning as everyone settled in for another long day of work.

"The dailies screening room was always a real white-knuckler—especially if you had a shot up for approval," says Buck Buckley. "It wasn't unusual to see a couple of people coming out of there in tears." In the dailies screening room, Selick sat in the center of the crowd, with the back two rows reserved for the animators. Other various crew members also attended dailies, including production managers and other department heads, camera people, and the director of photography, Pete Kozachik.

The tension was palpable as the standard countdown, known as the film leader, played before the film rolled. Those with a shot on the chopping block were never quite sure if it would land with the audience. The frame grabber allowed the animator to review just the last three frames they shot, so it wasn't guaranteed that the entire shot as a whole would look perfect on the big screen. "I often describe a movie like *Nightmare*, where we had virtually no video storage, akin to doing a painting," explains Angie Glocka. "But a painting where the artist is unable to see anything but the brushstrokes she happens to be working on at the moment, and then is never able to view the finished painting until the opening of the art show!"

The animators watched their shots with breathless anticipation, hoping for Selick's coveted thumbs-up. "There were always worries about potential technical flaws, like something being bumped accidentally on the set or a light burning out unnoticed," animator Joel Fletcher recalls.

The difference between a successful shot and one that needed extra work was often very obvious based on the energy in the room. "If the shot was approved, there would be applause," says Anthony Scott. "If there was silence or the phrase 'Let's see it cut in' [cut into the current edit of the film], then you knew there was a potential problem with the shot."

If this was only a pop-through, the time lost was minimal, and the animator could head back to the stage and refine the shot. But a direction to reshoot footage that was intended to be final was devastating for an animator—not only because of the time and effort wasted, but the inevitable negative stamp it put on their work. "You have to endure the reshoot, get through it, and get out on the other side," Buckley says. "Reshoot is one step to being out the door."

Some animators inserted gags into their shots just to have a bit of fun with dailies. Whereas some were harmless, a gag could be costly if Henry Selick wasn't a fan. Angie Glocka recalls adding a gag shot in her animation of the little blond boy who screams when his Christmas tree is eaten by a giant snake. Glocka tried adding a few frames of the little boy wetting his pants as he's screaming, which she considered too good to pass up. The gag was a hit in dailies, but it sadly wasn't included in the final cut. "In hindsight it's really dangerous, because what if your shot didn't work and then you have a gag at the end? It's a catastrophe. I probably would never do anything like that again!" Glocka says. The fact that some animators still snuck some fun into dailies, despite the nerves and high stakes, is a testament to how supportive and lighthearted this amazing crew was.

PAGE 104: Sally with her many replacement faces and eyelids.

PAGE 105: A member of the puppet fabrication crew bringing one of Sally's many faces to life.

BELOW: The sign marking the entry to Christmas Town.

OPPOSITE TOP: The Mayor and other Halloween Town residents during the "Making Christmas" number.

OPPOSITE BOTTOM: Jack Skellington conducting experiments to understand Christmas.

TOP FIVE TRICKY PUPPETS

Not every puppet was created equal on the set of Tim Burton's The Nightmare Before Christmas. Here were the top offenders, as ranked by votes from the animators themselves:

ZERO: There were several reasons why the full-scale Zero puppet was not very animator-friendly—the first being the nature of its on-screen appearance. Zero was animated using two different techniques to give him his ghostly transparency. The first technique—called the "Pepper's ghost" technique after John Pepper, the man who popularized it in 1862 for the theater—was to animate Zero on the side of the set via a "limbo background," which was essentially just a simple black cloth. The puppet's image was then reflected into the set using what's known in optical effects as a "beam splitter" or half-silvered mirror. If this wasn't complicated enough, the effects team also used the double exposure technique for some shots (see "Stop-Mo Terms to Know: Double Exposure," page 93). Zero's puppet was also inherently dangerous—it was made of a sheet of toxic lead, so protective gloves were needed when handling him. If the animator didn't get Zero's wavelike movements just right, the sheet of lead got kinks in it, and if they were worked too many times, it could crack. The friendly little ghost dog was a great addition to the film, but not exactly an animator's best friend on set.

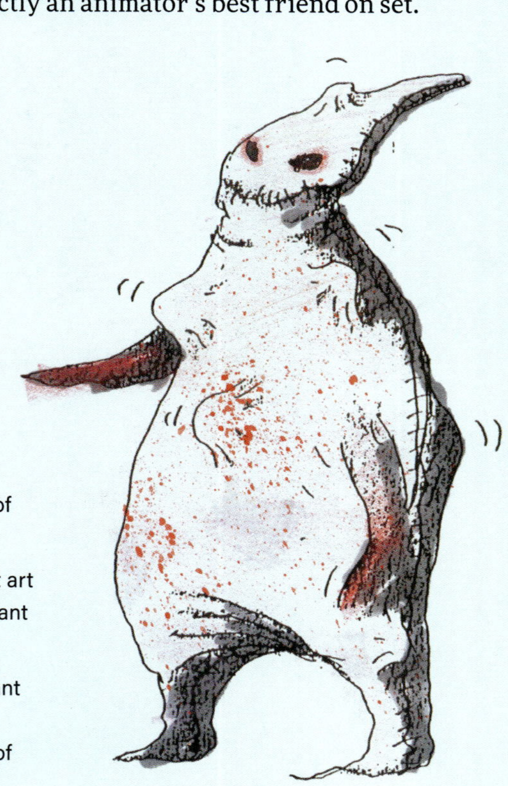

THIS PAGE: Concept art of Oogie Boogie.

OPPOSITE LEFT: Concept art of Sally by visual consultant Rick Heinrichs.

OPPOSITE RIGHT: Assistant art director Kendal Cronkhite's concept art of Sally.

OOGIE BOOGIE: Oogie Boogie's evil antics were not exclusive to the story—his puppet stirred up trouble for the animators as well. He was notoriously tough to animate due to his enormous size, as he was double the size of an average puppet at a whopping twenty-four inches tall. Oogie Boogie's armature had to be kept very tight to support his heavy foam body, or it would flop downward. This was a major inconvenience when the armature needed to be a little loose to make the character's movements appear fluid and natural. To get Oogie to dance, the animator had to use a scalpel to carefully cut a small, inconspicuous hole into the side of the puppet to reach an Allen wrench inside to loosen the screw of his armature. To say Oogie Boogie didn't "play fair" on set is definitely an understatement.

SALLY: Although Sally was a beautiful puppet, she wasn't a favorite to animate for a few reasons. Sally's "slab of meat" hair had no movement, and it was difficult to get it to hang properly when she moved her head. She also had tiny hands, which made holding objects complicated, and her dress often restricted her movement as well. It's a wonder that so many amazing shots came out of these difficulties, really proving the animation team's high level of skill. Praise goes to animators Trey Thomas and Tim Hittle, who were named by several people as the animators who cracked the code of bringing this delicate rag doll to life.

THE MAYOR: The Mayor's tiny legs and feet, the only things holding up his rotund body, made him very difficult to animate without damaging the puppet. "Any time an animator had to move that puppet and make it walk, they'd have to be grabbing onto those teeny tiny ankles, and the foam right near the ankle would just fall apart," character fabricator Elise Robertson explains. The Mayor was constantly in the "puppet hospital," and his body shape required quick thinking on the part of the animators to get him to do basic movements like walking up stairs. Despite these challenges, the Mayor did get a vote for favorite character of the film by animator Mike Belzer. "I definitely have a soft spot for the Mayor," Belzer says. "Primarily because I think he's a cool character and Glenn Shadix did an amazing job with the voice."

THE VAMPIRES: The four vampire puppets weren't even sculpted to be in the final film. Rick Heinrichs created them as "study maquettes," or test sculptures, but they were given screen time as more minor characters were needed in certain scenes. The maquettes had a jointed body, but their arms were made only out of simple wire. They were much smaller in size than the rest of the puppets, but with a cast of characters of all shapes and sizes, the team decided to just keep them as is and not mold final versions. The vampire puppets' basic build proved tricky when they had to do a simple action like clapping because of the lack of tension, or springiness, of the wire. Their little hands couldn't stay together without bending one of their fingers around a finger on the other hand to get them to appear to properly clap.

Who was everyone's favorite puppet to animate? It was pretty much unanimously the star of the show, Jack Skellington. His armature was smooth and his clothing and latex "flesh" were minimal, so he was as close to animating a bare armature as you can get in a stop-motion film.

EDITORIAL

When it comes to the editing process, and postproduction in general, *Tim Burton's The Nightmare Before Christmas* is more of a history lesson than an instruction manual. The movie was shot on film rather than digitally, and so the editing process differed greatly from a modern-day stop-motion feature. Today, stop-motion films use digital cameras, capture footage in a drive, and use video editing software, which takes care of everything from rearranging scenes to color correction. The process of editing on *Nightmare* is called linear editing because the order of the frames is predetermined in a sequence. Nonlinear editing, or digital video editing, allows the editor to access and rearrange frames in any order. Many of the tasks that the *Nightmare* editing team performed are now completely obsolete. This makes the amount of work the editors did that much more impressive.

The film was edited by essentially two people, Stan Webb and Edie Ichioka, plus a few apprentice or assistant editors who came and went. Once the film was shot and developed by local developer Monaco Film Labs, it found its way to the editing room and the Steenbeck flatbed editor, the most common film editing tool from the 1950s to the 1990s. Looking like a table with flat rotating plates to put both the reel of film and the soundtrack laid on their side, the Steenbeck allows both the picture and sound to be played simultaneously as the editors review each frame on a screen. In the case of *Nightmare*, the film was often reviewed on the flatbed with the director, animator(s), and production management crew standing by.

In linear editing, when it's determined by the editor and director that a frame of film needs to be cut, the edge number (the number printed on each frame of film) is typically noted, and the film is removed from the flatbed. The editor then physically cuts the 35mm film with a blade, removes the frame of film not needed, and puts the rest of the film back together using a tape splicer. A tape splicer is a small machine that joins two pieces of film together using a piece of clear tape. The tape is transparent, and it usually only covers the two frames of film that it connects together. If a tape splice is done properly, the edited roll of film should have no trouble feeding through a projector, and the cut appears totally seamless when the film is viewed. However, to prevent damaging the film, editors avoid making too many cuts or removing a piece of tape after the glue has been stuck for too long.

OPPOSITE TOP: The Steenbeck flatbed editor, the gold standard for linear editing from the 1950s to 1990s.

OPPOSITE BOTTOM: Concept art of Lock, Shock, and Barrel.

STOP-MO TERMS TO KNOW

POSTPRODUCTION: Everything that happens after the animation of the film is complete. This includes editorial, scoring, sound design and mixing, and special effects.

STORYBOARD: A rough outline of a film in which essential frames are illustrated on individual sheets of paper and lined up in succession.

STORY REEL: A rough draft of the film made up of temporary shots until final animation is swapped in as it's completed; also called a work reel or animatic. It can include storyboards, scratch or final dialogue, and sound effects and music.

Although the process of editing on a flatbed is the same for live-action and stop-motion, the editorial decisions can be very different. *Nightmare* editor Stan Webb describes editing for live action as "almost like sculpting stone . . . animation is an *additive* process, where it's more like sculpting with clay. You're really creating a movie in editorial before you go into production, rather than editing it after production."

Since *Nightmare* was shot on film, Webb had to be much more careful with the slicing blade than if he'd been working digitally with editing software such as Avid, Final Cut, or Adobe Premiere. A crucial misstep in the editing room or mishandling the film in any way could result in costly reshoots—something nobody wanted to explain to the director. Due to the pressure, Webb had a recurring nightmare while working on the film that the developer, Monaco Film Labs, was burning down with all of their film inside. The film roll was a particularly sacred object in Skellington Productions, and rightfully so, as all of the hours spent on *Nightmare* would be for nothing if anything was to ever happen to it. During production, there was only one copy!

THE FINAL FILM

On February 21, 1993, *Tim Burton's The Nightmare Before Christmas* wrapped production. There were still a few lingering special effects that needed to be completed, but because stop-motion animation relies on what is captured on camera, the film was already largely complete. Everyone had a sense that what they had done was innovative, unique, and compelling, particularly as it embraced Burton's initial vision even after two years of development and evolution. It was a singular experience for the filmmakers.

"It was so much fun, like an adventure every day," the film's artistic coordinator Allison Abbate reflects. "When you're shooting on film, you never know if the shot came through until you see it projected. So, you'd be sitting in dailies at seven o'clock in the morning and just biting your nails hoping that a light didn't turn off or something didn't fall unnoticed in the background of the shot. That kind of stress bonds you with the team. It's like being in a war together. When it works, it is an amazing feeling, and I think we've all been chasing that high for the rest of our lives."

"It was just a remarkable group of people," adds Trey Thomas. "I've worked on a bunch of movies and that group was the most symbiotic. Everybody had each other's back, working toward one goal. It's never happened since. I've been on a lot of great, fun movies, but there was a cohesiveness on [*Nightmare*] that you can't design—it just happens. I think we all look back on it as one of the big highlights, if not the highlight, of our careers."

RIGHT: Jack and Sally come together atop Spiral Hill in the final scene of the film.

HALLOWEENLAND

CHAPTER 7

BURTON'S POWERFUL RECURRING *NIGHTMARE*

"Some of the Halloween creatures might be a tad scary for smaller children, but this is the kind of movie older kids will eat up; it has the kind of offbeat, subversive energy that tells them wonderful things are likely to happen."

—ROGER EBERT ON *TIM BURTON'S THE NIGHTMARE BEFORE CHRISTMAS* (OCTOBER 22, 1993)

When *Tim Burton's The Nightmare Before Christmas* first arrived in theaters in October of 1993, audiences were unsure what to make of it. Was it a Halloween movie or a Christmas movie? Was it for kids or adults? Was it a musical or a horror film? The film didn't look or sound like recent Walt Disney Studios animated features, such as *The Little Mermaid* (1989). It was being released via Touchstone Pictures, a distributor that typically unleashed more mature fare (such as *Pretty Woman*, 1990). It was also an outlier alongside other contemporary popular movies: Beloved family flicks in 1993 included more conventional stories like *The Sandlot* and *The Secret Garden*, but this, the story of a misfit skeleton seeking his place in a fantastical world, was less easily defined, making it more challenging to sell to audiences.

WHAT'S THIS?: DEFINING THE UNDEFINABLE

The feature premiered in New York City on October 13th, 1993, followed by the general release on October 29th, 1993. There was also a star-studded event on Halloween for the release of the picture book *The Nightmare Before Christmas*, attended by Burton, Catherine O'Hara, and even Phil Collins, who brought along a young Lily Collins, dressed as a princess.

"They thought the movie was very dark and would scare little kids," producer Denise Di Novi recalls about Disney's decision to release the film as part of Touchstone Pictures. "It is darker than the average animated movie. It's hard to believe now, but when we made *Batman Returns*, people thought, 'Oh my, it's so dark and disturbing.' If you watch it now, it's so tame compared to the Batman movies that came after. It shows you how times have changed. But Disney thought *Nightmare* was too scary for little kids."

Even amid Disney's concerns, *Tim Burton's The Nightmare Before Christmas* earned a modest $51 million at the box office and garnered positive reviews from critics. Roger Ebert praised the film's innovation and uniqueness, writing, "One of the many pleasures of *Tim Burton's The Nightmare Before Christmas* is that there is not a single recognizable landscape within it. Everything looks strange and haunting. Even Santa Claus would be difficult to recognize without his red-and-white uniform." Peter Travers added in *Rolling Stone* that the film "has the earmarks of an enduring classic. Of all the new Halloween films, only this one has the power to truly haunt our dreams."

PAGE 114: Concept art of Jack as the Pumpkin King.

BOTTOM: Concept art of Jack playing as Santa Claus in a hearse-shaped sleigh.

OPPOSITE: Art by Tim Burton depicting Jack dressed as Santa Claus, complete with skeleton reindeer.

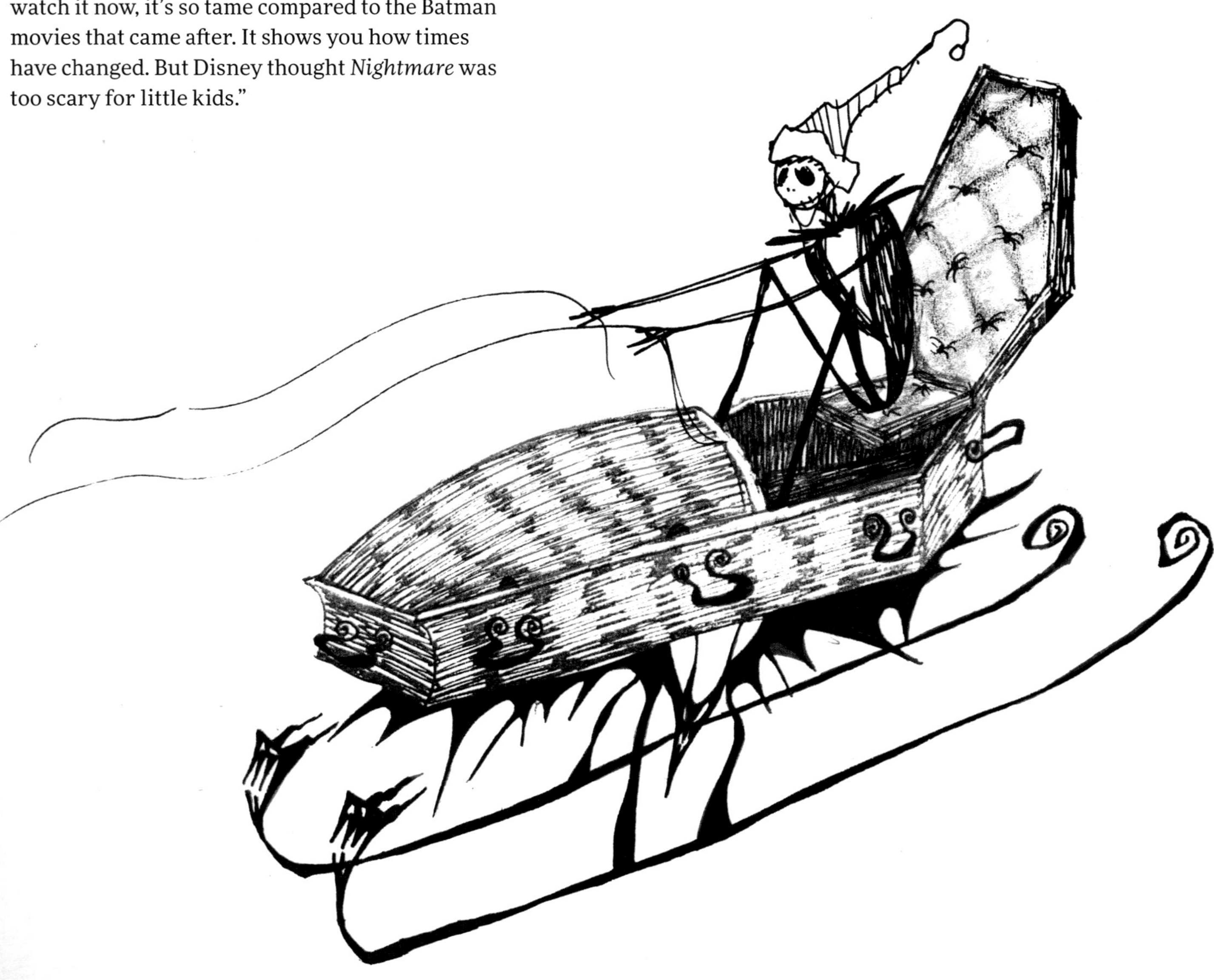

Despite some modest promotion, including bus-stop ads and a Burger King campaign, the response to the film was relatively tepid. "It was highly regarded for its visual audacity and for the lively story," Chris Sarandon says. "But I don't recall there being this big groundswell, a *Star Wars* kind of response to a movie. It was muted. It didn't blow up. But it's certainly blown up over time."

For the filmmakers, there was a sense of disappointment as the movie came and went. The crew had spent two years meticulously crafting the world of Halloween Town and its inhabitants, and once it disappeared from theaters there was a sense that Jack Skellington and pals had vanished from the cultural zeitgeist. Although the film had built a small fan base, and some merchandise, including a "Bone Daddy" T-shirt, could be found in stores, *Tim Burton's The Nightmare Before Christmas* initially appeared to have been a fleeting creation.

"It came and went pretty quickly and didn't do very well," Elfman reflected around the film's twenty-fifth anniversary. "Nobody understood what it was or how to market it. I put so much into this project, including so much of my own personality, that it really hurt. At the time, I was really depressed after it came out. I put so much into it, and it was gone."

Henry Selick and Burton understood the initial reluctance of audiences to fill the theaters. *Tim Burton's The Nightmare Before Christmas* was an unusual movie, about unusual characters singing unusual songs. However, both filmmakers were certain the artistry and the vision were there. Despite the public's reaction, *Nightmare* had a soul that very few movies possess, and there was something about it that felt more important than simple box office numbers.

TOP: Early concept art by Tim Burton of the Hinterlands, featuring doors to the other lands.

OPPOSITE: Early art of Dr. Finkelstein done by assistant art director Bill Boes.

A GROWING AUDIENCE

OPPOSITE TOP: The case for the VHS edition of *Tim Burton's The Nightmare Before Christmas.*

OPPOSITE BOTTOM LEFT: A storyboard frame of Dr. Finkelstein.

OPPOSITE BOTTOM RIGHT: Concept art of the striped snake that eats an entire Christmas tree.

A lot of factors played into the gradual growth of the film's fan base, but for many the central reason is the film's original artistic vision. "There was a really simple thing: It is just really good," film historian Ian Nathan explains. "It's really charming and visually wonderful, so it just carries you along. And great films find their audience. That started to happen with *Tim Burton's The Nightmare Before Christmas*. People bought it on DVD and they started to watch it repeatedly."

Burton himself isn't completely sure what's been behind the ever-expanding phenomenon of the film. Like the making of the movie, attempting to understand *Nightmare*'s success has been like trying to capture lightning in a bottle. It's a once-in-a-lifetime occurrence that has ultimately been generated by the fans themselves. "I think it just had enough of a core thing and they rereleased it, and it gained traction," he says. "There are certain things that historically have happened that way, and it's hard to predict why, like *The Rocky Horror Picture Show*. I would look at it as, something to achieve is a holiday kind of thing that is sort of a perennial."

In 2000, Touchstone Home Video rereleased *Tim Burton's The Nightmare Before Christmas* as a special-edition DVD with bonus features, including audio commentary from Selick, a making-of feature, and deleted scenes. By the mid-2000s, Walt Disney Pictures, recognizing the immense fan base and the opportunities to grow the property, brought the film back under their official umbrella. The studio converted *Nightmare* to Disney Digital 3D and, on October 20, 2006, rereleased the film in theaters, with special presentations at the Venice Film Festival and the London Film Festival. It allowed a whole new audience to discover the movie, and for Burton, the 3D rerelease emphasized the hallmark magic of stop-motion film.

"I love things in 3D," he explains. "It took me back to when you're on the set looking at these puppets and the tactile nature of the sets. The 3D actually brought you more into what that world was like. In this particular case, I felt like it enhanced what the artists did—you could feel the texture of the puppets and I thought it was great. I loved it. You can't say that about everything, but for this it brought you closer to being on a set and feeling these characters. I was very happy with the outcome of that."

That stop-motion format is also part of the movie's enduring legacy. There's a tangible, handmade quality to the film, almost as though the viewer could reach out and touch the characters and their world. It allows the story to feel even more immersive and immediate, which helps it to stand out amid the computer-generated (CG) animation that has taken over Hollywood since its release.

"There is something to the idea that this thing actually exists," Henry Selick says. "Its flaws are in the animation and the imperfections are like a clue that it's real. You'd never have those with CG. You inherently know this exists and it was touched by humans."

Alongside its handmade artistry, the film showcases Burton's particular style. It's unusual for an animated work in Hollywood to reflect an individual vision, rather than that of a studio itself. The convergence of the filmmaker's singular style with Selick's careful skill and the crew's stop-motion prowess resulted in something completely standalone.

"Certainly, people respond to hand-drawn films and digitally created films with a lot of passion," associate producer Phil Lofaro notes. "But this is a film that is uniquely Tim Burton. You can't look at that film and not see his hand. None of the other animated films are really like that. Even with the hand-drawn stuff from Disney, nothing looks like one person's vision the way that *Nightmare* does."

"I don't want to be hyperbolic, but I think it's a masterpiece," Di Novi adds. "Who else besides Tim would interweave Halloween and Christmas like that? At the core, the emotionality of the character being so different and yearning to be accepted—which is in all of Tim's work—is always going to be meaningful to people. I think it's one of the greatest animated movies in history."

The constant rereleases, which have continued over the years in various forms, including a 4D version that incorporated additional elements like fog and snow into the viewing experience, have played into the growth of *Tim Burton's The Nightmare Before Christmas*. But the movie's popularity is also connected to that message of learning to belong. Although *Nightmare* was of its time when it was made, the story and its themes transcend a specific era or trend. Burton has always incorporated universal ideas into his films, but his fascination with an outcast finding acceptance felt especially poignant in a family-friendly, holiday film.

Many film historians and critics have pointed to that universality as one of the reasons *Nightmare* has continued to captivate audiences for generations. "The continuing popularity of this movie probably has something to do with its message," author Edwin Page wrote in *Gothic Fantasy: The Films of Tim Burton*. "It is about staying true to yourself, despite failures, despite misunderstanding. Through Jack's failure to bring seasonal goodwill the film also tells us that not everything in life will work out the way we want it to. This is an important message, especially for children who are often force fed 'happily ever after' endings that give them a false perspective on life. *Tim Burton's The Nightmare Before Christmas* presents something more real, though woven into a fantastical narrative."

Jack's story resonated with the filmmakers and crew as much as it resonates with fans. The emotional core of the film, along with the impressive artistry and tactile nature of the stop-motion craft, have allowed the movie to transcend generations. Against all odds, *Tim Burton's The Nightmare Before Christmas* has become the exact thing that inspired it in the first place—a recurrent holiday favorite.

"I would always get very excited as a child to watch those holiday films that created the sense of an event to me . . . an event that you look forward to on television," Burton says. "I wanted to create something that gave me the kinds of feelings I had when I was growing up watching those classics. I was always very proud of *Nightmare* and loved it, but at the time when it came out, it wasn't what it's turned into. It's been a journey to get there. It makes me happy because it took a long time for that to happen, but it was always something that I felt satisfied that instinct for me."

BELOW LEFT: Concept art of a cyclops monster.

BELOW RIGHT: Concept art of the Wolfman.

OPPOSITE: Concept art of the Corpse Mom.

EGGSALAD SANDWICH

NOVELS AND BOOKS

For many years, *Tim Burton's The Nightmare Before Christmas* was a standalone story. Even though the characters lived on in fan fiction and fan art, as well as games and merchandise, only recently has the tale of Jack Skellington and his friends continued in other forms. Though Burton has been approached to make a sequel to *Nightmare*, the filmmaker has always rejected the idea—especially in any form other than traditional stop-motion. Burton is, however, open to expanding the world of Halloween Town through games or novels when it makes sense, particularly if it allows a character or aspect of the story to be illuminated from a fresh perspective.

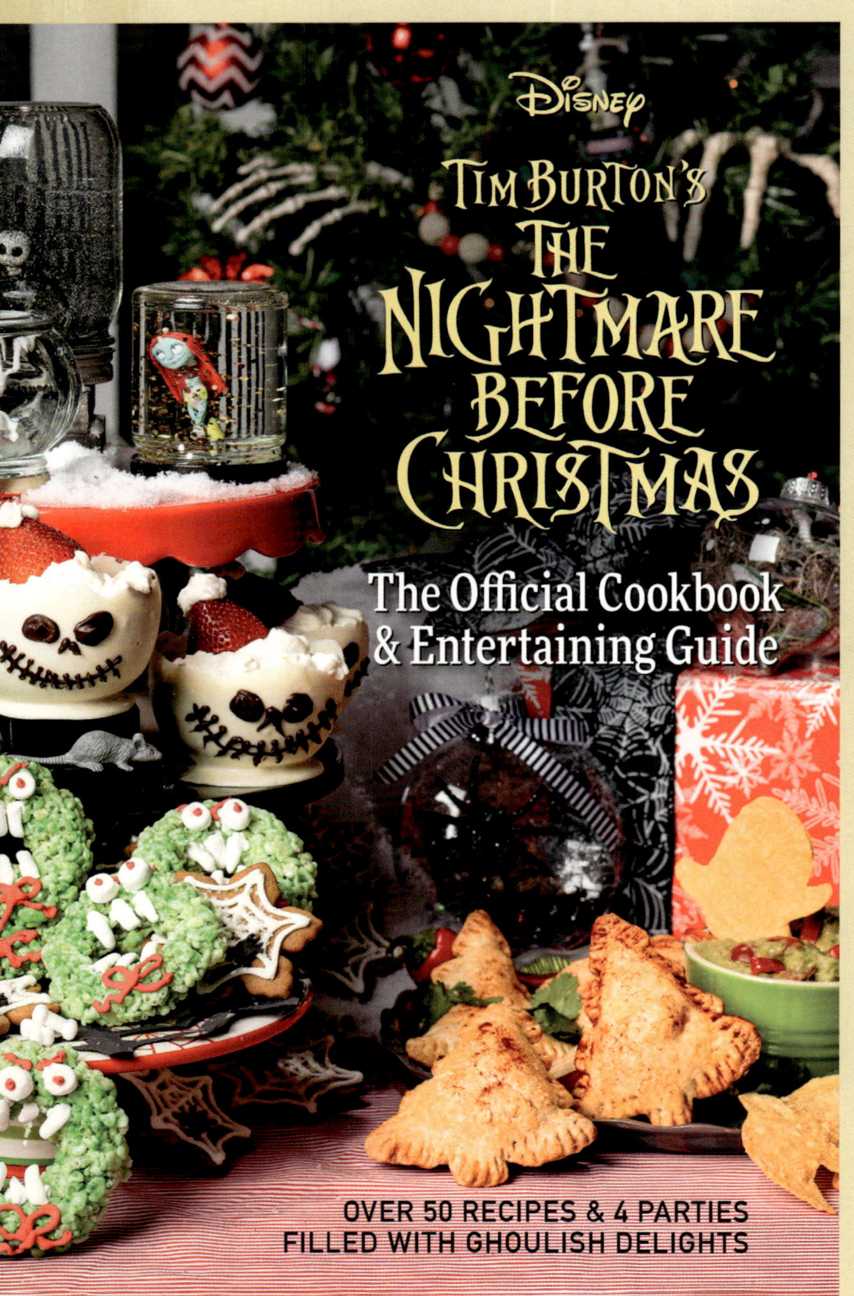

"I resisted doing sequels because it is what it is," Burton explains. "I want the film to exist rather than go, 'Let's have Jack go to Thanksgiving World or torment the Easter Bunny more or whatever.' There's a purity to it, and it goes back to the stop-motion, but the books and toys look at it in a different way. I didn't want to do a film like that because I felt it would take away from the purity of what the original is."

In 2020, Disney Manga released *Tim Burton's The Nightmare Before Christmas: Zero's Journey*, written by D.J. Milky and illustrated by Kei Ishiyama, David Hutchison, Dan Conner, and Kiyoshi Arai. In the comic, Zero goes missing from Halloween Town and is forced to find his way home via Christmas Town, offering a deeper look at Jack's trusty companion. Many of the film's characters, including the Mayor, Sally, and Lock, Shock, and Barrel, returned for the comic. Another manga series, *Tim Burton's The Nightmare Before Christmas: Mirror Moon*, ran for five issues from 2021 until 2022. Written by Mallory Reaves with artwork by Gabriella Chianello and Nataliya Torretta, the series centered on Sally as she took over Halloween planning for Jack. This one also featured familiar characters from the film, such as the beloved vampires.

The most significant expansion of *Tim Burton's The Nightmare Before Christmas* arrived in 2022 with *Long Live the Pumpkin Queen*, a young adult novel by writer Shea Ernshaw. The book follows after the events of *Nightmare*, shifting the perspective to Sally, who has recently married Jack, and detailing her adventures in the newly discovered Dream Town.

"The whole story came to me all at once," Ernshaw says. "I had this notion of Sally and Jack, and wanting to see what happens with their relationship. In the movie, we get to see Jack and the nightmare that he creates on Christmas Eve. I thought, 'Well, the juxtaposition of nightmares is dreams.' I knew it needed to be a story about dreams, so naturally, the Sandman was going to be the villain. I also wanted to explore more of Sally's background and her origin."

Although Sally is an essential character in the film, viewers learn more about Jack than they do about the practical and persistent rag doll, who was originally crafted by screenwriter Caroline Thompson. In the novel, Sally's history and her true parents are revealed, as well as her own hopes and dreams for the future. For Ernshaw, *Long Live the Pumpkin Queen* is a way for Sally to finally be the protagonist after all these years.

"I kept coming back to who Sally was and the stories I think she would have wanted to tell," Ernshaw says. "I really tried to be true to her. That was a question I asked myself as I was writing: Is this really Sally? Is this what Sally would want? She's waited a really long time to have the story told, so I wanted to do it justice and give her the story she deserved." This expansion of the story resonated with fans. In a continuation of Sally's adventures, a sequel to *Long Live the Pumpkin Queen* published in July 2025.

Sally's story continues to grow along with *Nightmare*'s enormous popularity—even if it isn't exactly canon. In October 2024, Disney Publishing released a new entry into its *New York Times* bestselling A Twisted Tale series and author Mari Mancusi released *Sally's Lament*, which asked the question, "What if *Sally* discovered Christmas Town instead of Jack Skellington?" Although the situation is reversed, the main *Nightmare* characters remain very true to themselves.

"The nice thing about the A Twisted Tale [series] is that you're playing with the same characters in the same world. It's not like Sally could suddenly be evil or change her personality; everyone has to be the same characters that they are in the original film. It's more of a plot twist," Mancusi says. "For this particular one, when Jack is in the graveyard, singing he's unhappy and unsatisfied with everything and wishes there was something more, she is watching him in the film. It kind of goes on from there and he finds Christmas Town. But in [*Sally's Lament*], she accidentally knocks over a gravestone and stumbles out. He discovers her in the cemetery and she says, 'Jack, I know exactly what you mean.' Jack starts to feel better talking to Sally, and he goes home, so she's the one that ends up going into the Hinterlands by following Zero, who flies out there and ends up on the adventure."

Mancusi describes that as well as film favorites such as Jack, Sally and Zero, there are also several brand-new characters not seen in the original *Nightmare*, and that Sally spends a lot more time in Christmas Town than Jack ever did. "It seems like everything in Christmas Town is so jolly and nice and everything, and then Sally starts to realize there's a dark undertone to it. Another thing you'll find is a lot more Jack and Sally romance than you did in the film. I really love the idea of them getting together, so I was able to concentrate on that a lot more."

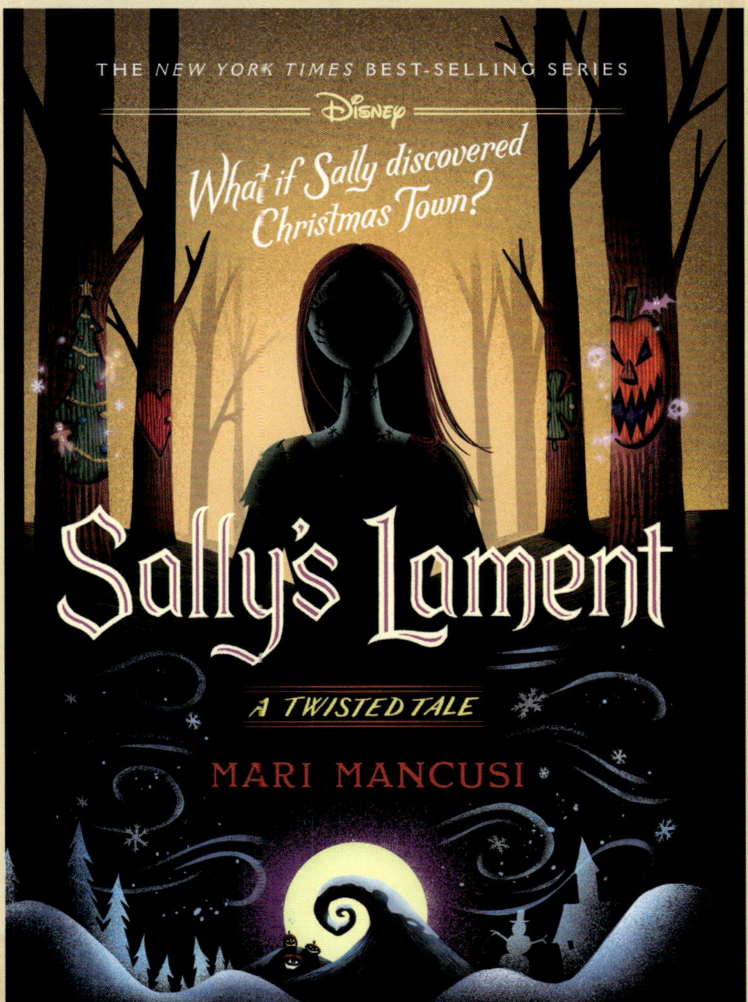

A YEAR-ROUND HOLIDAY

The debate as to whether *Tim Burton's The Nightmare Before Christmas* is a Halloween movie or a Christmas movie rages on decades later. Many people embrace the film as an annual tradition around both holidays, but there's no denying its strong connection with Halloween. While growing up in Burbank, Burton was obsessed with both holidays, often decorating his Christmas tree with Halloween-inspired ornaments. To the filmmakers, there's a similar spirit that connects both events.

"Halloween was my favorite, and it always seemed to be the festive season from Halloween to Christmas," Burton remembers. "So, it's an extended holiday to me, so to speak, and in my house Christmas and Halloween got jumbled up. I kept Halloween going. I always enjoyed the light of Christmas, but Halloween was a bit darker, and that's where the juxtaposition of things in the film came from."

Prior to *Nightmare*'s 1993 theatrical release, there were a few Halloween films beloved by moviegoing audiences. *The Rocky Horror Picture Show* had come out in 1975 and transformed into a holiday classic, but it was largely for a mature audience. *Nightmare* offered something new for those who loved eerie things with a less terrifying feel, as did its contemporary *Hocus Pocus*, released the same year.

"I think *Nightmare* helped to restore some of Halloween's whimsical quality, especially in regards to its cinematic portrayals," explains author Lisa Morton. "Halloween is a festival that has been impacted by film before—John Carpenter's 1978 classic *Halloween* helped steer Halloween celebrations more toward adults—but *Nightmare* appealed to many fans of the holiday by emphasizing playfulness, joy, and creativity."

The popularity of the film as a holiday tradition was aided by the fact that there was nothing else like it for either Halloween or Christmas. "It's not a traditional Christmas film or holiday film," says Brian Volk-Weiss, director of the series *The Holiday Movies That Made Us*. "It can be a scary movie, depending on your age. But there are a lot of incredibly sophisticated, complicated characters and personalities. The plot itself is extremely simple, but the characters in the plot are so complicated."

The intersection of Halloween and Christmas in *Tim Burton's The Nightmare Before Christmas* is obvious. Yet since its release, the film has evolved into a classic viewing for Valentine's Day, Easter, Thanksgiving, and more recent semi-holidays like Halfway to Halloween and Halfway to Christmas. These holidays fit in with the original story, too: Jack is the Pumpkin King of Halloween Town and involves himself in the holiday of Christmas, but numerous holiday doorways exist in the Hinterlands, and the Easter Bunny has a small but essential role in the film. Although *Nightmare* may have initially cemented itself as a specific annual tradition, throughout the past decade it has also become a 365-day celebration.

This expansion has been aided by several factors, including extensive and constant merchandising and the film's frequent presence at various fan conventions, including San Diego Comic-Con, which takes place yearly in July. "Comic-Con was a huge gateway for fans," notes Elise Barkan, former Director of Global Franchise Development & Marketing at Disney Parks, Experiences and Products. "Once we saw the success at Comic-Con, we showed up with *Tim Burton's The Nightmare Before Christmas* in a whole host of ways."

Tim Burton's The Nightmare Before Christmas has trickled into celebrations for Valentine's Day thanks to Jack and Sally's memorable love story. Hallmark sells *Nightmare*-themed cards for couples. Many fans host Thanksgiving dinners inspired by the world of the film, a fact that is less surprising than one might initially assume. Several writers and film critics, in fact, have argued that *Nightmare* is actually a Thanksgiving movie. According to Alison Foreman's Mashable article in 2021, "Jack Skellington's harrowing journey from Pumpkin King to disgraced Santa imposter seriously lends itself to Thanksgiving's themes of gratefulness and family . . . Ultimately, they're what this animated classic is really about."

For many, it makes complete sense that *Tim Burton's The Nightmare Before Christmas* has found a year-round audience. "The film resonates with so many people, so they make it their own," explains George McClements, Director of

PAGE 124: Cover of *Tim Burton's The Nightmare Before Christmas: The Official Cookbook & Entertaining Guide*, a book offering recipes and entertaining ideas based on the film.

PAGE 125 TOP: Cover of *Long Live the Pumpkin Queen: Tim Burton's The Nightmare Before Christmas*, a book that follows Sally as she undergoes an adventure in the mysterious Dream Town.

PAGE 125 BOTTOM: The cover of *Sally's Lament: A Twisted Tale*, a story that reimagines Sally as the Halloween Town resident who discovers the snowy Christmas Town.

OPPOSITE TOP: Sally cooking with some mysterious potions, as seen in the final film.

OPPOSITE BOTTOM: Residents of Halloween Town, including the Wolfman and the Harlequin Demon, during a town meeting.

Concept Art and Story Development at Disney Parks, Experiences and Products. "The fact that we see the turkey door means that Jack can go to Thanksgiving Town. The fact that we see the four-leaf clover means he can go to St. Patrick's Day Town. And obviously, Jack is going to go. He's not going to say 'I'm done' after he visits Christmas Town. He's not that character. So that's why we celebrate all year."

Perhaps the most meaningful aspect of a holiday like Thanksgiving or Christmas is the gathering of friends and family around a common table to enjoy a communal meal. Even for Halloween, with its tradition of trick-or-treating, food is a focal point—usually in the form of candy or sweets. Because these celebrations are so closely linked with cooking and dining, *Nightmare* often inspires the holiday meal itself. In fact, several cookbooks have been released for the fans of the film, encouraging home chefs to incorporate the aesthetic and themes of the movie into their holiday spreads. One such cookbook is *The Nightmare Before Christmas: The Official Cookbook & Entertaining Guide*. Released in 2021, features recipes and party-planning ideas for fans. It's not for the faint of heart, though: Dishes include Dr. Finkelstein Bite-Sized "Brain" Puff Pies and Oogie Boogie Pasta Worms.

Jack, Sally, and the Halloween Town crew have cemented themselves in pop culture in numerous ways, but none so obvious as the elaborate Halloween costumes worn by the film's most famous fans. Since the release of *Tim Burton's The Nightmare Before Christmas*, everyone from Gwen Stefani to Channing Tatum to Joey King have dressed as the characters to celebrate Halloween. Many of the costumes have been custom creations, with makeup, wigs, and masks to match, and each one has had a unique flair. One of the most memorable interpretations of one of Tim Burton's characters was in 2011, when actress Michelle Trachtenberg attended Heidi Klum's annual Halloween party dressed as "Blue Girl With Wine," the eponymous character of Tim Burton's 1997 painting that evokes his original concept sketches for Sally. Melissa Joan Hart, Nicole Richie, Vanessa Hudgens, and Austin Butler have all joined the fun over the years.

Though most of the notable costumes have been worn as part of Halloween, some celebrities have brought the world of *Nightmare* to other celebrations throughout the years as well. Khloé Kardashian and Kendall Jenner dressed as Sally and Jack for their nephew Mason Disick's fourth birthday, which was themed around the film, in 2014, whereas Ariana Grande donned a Jack Skellington-inspired ensemble onstage in 2015. Rita Ora also wore a *Nightmare* homage at the 2013 Parklife Festival in Manchester, England. It's clear that love for Burton's creation extends far and wide.

IN THE PARKS

With *Nightmare*'s increasing appeal, it was only a matter of time before Jack and Sally would visit the Disney Parks. On October 5, 2001, Haunted Mansion Holiday arrived at Disneyland. The annual overlay, which takes over the iconic attraction each fall from Halloween through January without impacting the original attraction's structure, was conceived in the late 1990s. Says Henry Selick, "When the Haunted Mansion at Disneyland was transformed into a *Nightmare* extravaganza, we then felt we were truly loved by the Disney label."

"It was very clear that this audience were huge fans of *Tim Burton's The Nightmare Before Christmas*, but perhaps there wasn't enough momentum for a standalone *Nightmare Before Christmas* attraction," explains Todd Martens, a Los Angeles–based journalist who has written extensively about Disneyland and the Disney Parks in general. "But there was enough momentum to redo Haunted Mansion for the holidays. At Disneyland this is something that happens with more regularity than at Walt Disney World, in part because Disneyland is a locals' park. It was Disney recognizing that *Nightmare* had become an important cult film and that its audience was gravitating toward Disneyland and the Haunted Mansion."

The concept also came about after Disney's Imagineers asked themselves what sort of holiday celebration might occur in the beloved attraction. "We were walking by Haunted Mansion one day and we were like, 'Oh, what if Santa landed on that house? What might it be?'" explained Walt Disney Imagineering's Steve Davison. "And that's really how it all was born." He added, "Artistically, it was a big challenge because you have two opposing forces: You have the Haunted Mansion, which has a very classic design, and then you have the *Nightmare* style."

The intention wasn't necessarily to re-create the film as a Disney Parks attraction. Instead, the Imagineers wanted to draw on beloved elements of the movie, including the Christmas countdown clock, Jack's sleigh, the vampire teddy bear, and Zero, and bring them into the Haunted Mansion in an organic way. The film inspired much of the design, which feels like a logical extension of Halloween Town. "The colors were all predetermined for us, because when you look at the film it's all orange, purple, black, red," noted illustrator Tim Wollweber, who created many of the visual elements in the overlay. "It was just putting that all together to make these wacky patterns and pointy skulls."

LEFT AND OPPOSITE: Photos from the Oogie Boogie Bash, which occurs annually at Disney California Adventure Park in Anaheim, California.

MISTER
OOGIE
BOOGIE
LIVE

A focal point of the attraction's overlay is Spiral Hill, which is covered in snow and dozens of glowing pumpkin heads. The mountain, which dangles with icicles, towers over guests inside the attraction. It's another example of how the Imagineers took the film and made it their own. "The concept for the snow mountain, of course, came from the film," explained Brian Sandahl, former art director of Haunted Mansion Holiday, adding, "We're not trying to recreate the movie. We're inspired by the movie, so we're taking that big piece that is very familiar to people that know the film inside and out, and we stuck that in the graveyard."

Many of the film's actors, notably Chris Sarandon, Ken Page, and Catherine O'Hara, reprised their character voices for the attraction. During the first year, the experience was soundtracked with a new score from composer Gordon Goodwin, but by 2002, a new soundtrack by John Debney, based on Danny Elfman's film score, could be heard throughout the rooms. The Haunted Mansion Holiday was such a success that a version of the attraction premiered in Tokyo Disneyland as the Haunted Mansion Holiday Nightmare. The overlay was similar to that in California, with many of the same elements, including the custom gingerbread house in the Grand Hall that changes each year. Both parks offer special merchandise sold in honor of the attraction and many fans visit the immersive experience more than once over the holiday season.

As the fan base of the film has grown, so has its popularity in the parks—and vice versa. "Millions of people a year go to Disneyland," Martens says. "If one of the signature attractions in the park has a makeover based on this Tim Burton film, anybody who has not seen that film goes home and watches it. People love the Haunted Mansion. They want to know the story of that attraction inside and out. They want to know anything that happens to it. Putting *Tim Burton's The Nightmare Before Christmas* in that attraction puts [it] into one of the most popular rides in the resort. And over the years, it has helped to turn *Nightmare* into a Disney classic that today would be regarded as important to the Disney collection of films as any of the other animated films that are represented throughout the park."

Elsewhere in the parks, guests can meet Jack and Sally throughout the year. But it's really around Halloween when *Tim Burton's The Nightmare Before Christmas* takes over the various theme parks. Even the film's bug-filled baddie got his own annual celebration starting in 2019. On select evenings every September and October, Oogie Boogie Bash – A Disney Halloween Party gathers Disney villains like the Queen from *Snow White and the Seven Dwarfs* (1937), Captain Hook from *Peter Pan* (1953), Cruella De Vil from *One Hundred and One Dalmatians* (1961), Ursula from *The Little Mermaid* (1989), and others for a sinister soiree inside Disney California Adventure Park at Disneyland. The park's Redwood Creek Challenge Trail undergoes a spooky upgrade and becomes Villains Grove, a portal Oogie Boogie uses to welcome Disney's nefarious ne'er-do-wells to his frightening festival. Though it's a bash for all the villains, Oogie Boogie is the ringleader, and he is often found along the "treat trails" where guests can actually trick-or-treat in the park. The nighttime event features a parade, themed games, and live performances by Disney Parks characters, villain and hero alike. Fans of all ages are encouraged to dress up in costume to trick-or-treat throughout the park.

At Walt Disney World in Orlando, Florida, *Nightmare* characters appear every year at Mickey's Not-So-Scary Halloween Party in the Magic Kingdom, and Jack dressed as Santa often pops up during annual events at Walt Disney World's Haunted Mansion and Disneyland Paris's Phantom Manor. In 2023, Disney's Hollywood Studios joined in the frightful fun with Disney Jollywood Nights, a holiday celebration featuring "What's This? Tim Burton's The Nightmare Before Christmas Sing-Along" in the Hyperion Theater. Other popular events at the Disney Parks throughout the year include Halfway to Halloween, held in the spring leading up to May 4. All year, however, guests can don a pair of *Nightmare*-themed mouse ears featuring Sally's colorful patchwork design or an eerie bat with black-and-white pinstripes—perfect for evoking the holiday spirit in any month.

"*The Nightmare Before Christmas* has become the backbone of Disney's Halloween events," says Martens. "I think each year you start to see greater proliferation. If you go to Disney California Adventure any time from late September through the end of Halloween, the first thing you see when you walk into that gate is Oogie Boogie. You hear his voice echoing throughout the park. You hear his laughter. There is a huge hunger for *Nightmare* among Disney theme park fans that continues to grow."

OPPOSITE: Concept art of the glow-in-the-dark bats that inhabit Oogie Boogie's lair.

WE KNOW JACK PODCAST

Over the years, many of the crew members who worked on *Tim Burton's The Nightmare Before Christmas* have stayed in touch. The film remains a powerful touchpoint in their lives and careers all these years later. They've held reunions and crew parties, including for the film's twenty-fifth anniversary, and some have continued to collaborate on other projects. But one of the most important documents of their continuing adoration for the movie is *We Know Jack*, a podcast created in 2019 by production coordinator Kat Alioshin and set builder Todd Lookinland. Each episode focuses on one member of the Nightmare crew, reflecting back on what it was like to work in Skellington Productions for two years.

"I can say, without hesitation, that I've never worked on a project before or since that was more exciting, more fun, or with everybody pulling in the same direction more," Lookinland says. "Everybody wanted to be there. With the podcast, we were trying to answer the questions of 'Why was this so magical? How do you re-create it? How come it's so hard to re-create a situation like this?' There's no real answer that we've found other than we were lucky. We were just super fortunate to have been involved in this thing that just turned out to be super fun and super magical and super exciting."

We Know Jack features conversations with everyone from the film's editor Stan Webb to art director Deane Taylor to several of the animators, including Angie Glocka and Mike Belzer. The interviews are extremely detailed, with each participant sharing new behind-the-scenes stories and anecdotes about how the movie came together. It's a must-listen for any fan of the film.

"It's so fun to see people's reactions to hearing stories that they feel are very special and that they haven't heard before," Alioshin says. "And you wouldn't have heard them because they're coming from people's hearts. Someone we're interviewing will say 'I hadn't told anyone this before' and, to us, that is very cool."

CHAPTER 8

A MUSICAL LEGACY FIT FOR A PUMPKIN KING

"If there's one thing that's a music destroyer, it's logic: too thought-out, too intellectual, about what it should or shouldn't be doing."

—DANNY ELFMAN, COMPOSER AND SINGING VOICE OF JACK SKELLINGTON

Tim Burton's The Nightmare Before Christmas wouldn't exist without writer/composer Danny Elfman's dynamic, quirky musical numbers and emotional score. Known previously as the lead singer of American New Wave band Oingo Boingo, Elfman transitioned into film scoring with Burton's directorial debut, *Pee-wee's Big Adventure*, in 1985. That film launched a creative partnership that continues to this day. Elfman has composed music for nineteen projects with Burton across forty years, but it was *Nightmare* that truly solidified the collaborative dynamic between the two.

When Burton began toying with the idea of adapting his holiday poem into a feature-length film, he knew instinctually the story would be best told as a musical. The filmmaker approached Elfman with the concept, a few lyrical ideas, and some sketches, relying on the musician to create songs that would capture Jack Skellington's inner life and the film's unique stop-motion animation.

"Danny was one of the first people on board," Burton recalls. "He was doing music before there was a script. We would just talk about the story—I would say, 'This happens, that happens, and then that happens,' and he wrote an opera. It was a back-and-forth in that way. A lot of the script was developed based on the music. We had similar sensibilities and he was obviously like a character in it, so it was more organic. It wasn't, 'Here's the script, go.' He was instrumental in the development of the whole thing."

Completing ten songs in preproduction—almost half of the movie's run time—Elfman's musical numbers and score cues became the foundation of *Tim Burton's The Nightmare Before Christmas* and were used by screenwriter Caroline Thompson as a framework for the film's script. And because the main themes were already written, the background music, or "underscore," was pulled from that material. Neither Burton nor Elfman had ever written a musical, so there were no rules. Each song had come naturally, with the pair focused simply on not becoming trapped by what was popular at the time.

"For both of us, our sense of rhyming and meter came from somewhere between Edward Gorey and Dr. Seuss," Elfman says. "That's probably where I get much of my lyrical rhyming and rhythm from. But we didn't have any idea of how to begin. We did have a clear idea of what we didn't want to do: 'We don't want this to sound like a Disney musical or Broadway musical.' Other than that, we didn't know what we wanted it to sound like."

Over the years, the music of *Tim Burton's The Nightmare Before Christmas* has generated its own legacy. By the late 1990s and early 2000s, the songs took on new shape with cover versions and rereleases of the original soundtrack. There was a clear connection between musical artists in the punk, emo, hard rock, and goth music scenes, especially in the 2000s, and mainstream bands like Fall Out Boy, Slipknot, and blink-182 paid homage to *Nightmare* with tattoos, song lyrics, and fashion choices. Walt Disney Records tapped numerous artists, from Korn to Evanescence's Amy Lee to Panic! at the Disco, to record official reimaginings of the film's musical numbers. Elfman's lyrics spoke to a generation of introspective people who had grown up watching *Nightmare* as kids. By the 2010s, Elfman's songs had fully established themselves in pop culture. Over the past decade, *Tim Burton's The Nightmare Before Christmas* has been performed live in concert in multiple countries, creating memorable moments of togetherness for fans. The songs continue to be reinterpreted by artists of all genres, and have become classics themselves.

PAGE 132: Concept art of Christmas Town by assistant art director Kendal Cronkhite.

ABOVE: Jack singing during the "Jack's Lament" sequence.

OPPOSITE TOP: Jack introducing Christmas to the residents of Halloween Town.

OPPOSITE BOTTOM: Jack following his attempt to bring Christmas to the Real World.

Because Elfman didn't lean on a particular style or trend when composing the music, *Nightmare*'s songs retain a timeless feel that holds up alongside Hollywood's best movie musicals. The songwriter isn't exactly sure why his songs have taken on a life of their own. "When Tim and I were creating them they were just a bunch of crazy, weird songs of a noncontemporary style," he admits. "My goal was to write songs that could be written now, but they also could have been written in the '30s or in the '50s. To try to make it so you can't even put an era behind it—that was my objective. I didn't want them to sound contemporary because at that point I really did not like what Broadway and contemporary musicals were doing musically. It bored me. So all I cared about is that it didn't go into that territory. But at the same time, I was drawing on all these different influences.

"I have no idea what keeps them alive," Elfman adds, "but I don't think any songwriter ever does."

DEVELOPING THE SONGS

After Burton had approached Elfman about writing songs for a stop-motion feature version of "The Nightmare Before Christmas," the musician dove in immediately. He began writing songs in 1991, working in tandem with Burton. Elfman was inspired by Burton's concept and found it relatively easy to write the melodies and lyrics that began to frame Jack's adventure. "He had all of these great pictures and drawings, as well as lines and poems; fragments of stuff," he recalled. "I remember a number of times I pushed him out the door because I started hearing the songs in my head. I'd start right on that, and three days later I'd have a demo which I'd come back and play for him. Then we'd start the next part of the story."

STOP-MO TERMS TO KNOW

UNDERSCORE: The background music that plays throughout the whole film.

The songs, composed by Elfman in a makeshift studio in Caroline Thompson's Burbank house, came to life chronologically. Burton would recount part of the story, and then Elfman would write the next song. He wrote quickly because Selick and the crew had already begun to set up shop at Skellington Productions in San Francisco. As he worked, Elfman drew on multiple influences for the music, pulling on past time periods and vintage styles. Kurt Weill's *The Threepenny Opera*, Cole Porter, Gilbert and Sullivan, and Rodgers and Hammerstein were the most significant inspirations.

"Town Meeting Song," with its casual, conversational singing-slash-talking charm, felt to Elfman like "the kind of thing Cole Porter might have done ages ago." For the lively number "What's This?," which Jack sings as he discovers Christmas Town, Elfman looked back to the Victorian era. "When I was writing 'What's This?' I was definitely thinking of Gilbert and Sullivan's 'I Am the Very Model of a Modern Major,'" he says. "I wanted to write something that was a tongue twister. Quick, insistent, and tricky."

On "Oogie Boogie's Song," Elfman paid homage to Cab Calloway's 1931 song "Minnie The Moocher," which was performed in a 1932 Betty Boop cartoon of the same name (as well as other Calloway numbers). Notably, Oingo Boingo had once covered the musician's bluesy tune in their 1982 film *Forbidden Zone*. For Elfman, Broadway star Ken Page was the right singer to embody the swaggering villain's signature tune. "We auditioned a lot of Oogie Boogies," he notes. "And when I heard Ken I felt like, 'Oh my God, this is who I wrote it for.'"

At the time, Elfman was still in Oingo Boingo, his formative band, and he couldn't help but pull from his experience as the lead singer of a rock group. In fact, the film's opening number, "This Is Halloween," shares a lyric with an Oingo Boingo song, "Tender Lumplings." Many of Jack's musical moments drew on Elfman's own desires to begin the next chapter of his career.

"Even though it was clearly Tim's story, I was also telling my own story through Jack because it was very personal for me," Elfman says, "I wanted to get out of my band and I didn't know how to do it. I felt a lot of obligation and guilt. So, as I was writing Jack's lyrics, even though I didn't contribute anything to the storyline, I was adding my own emotional sense to the character: Trying to find a way out of something that was hard to escape."

OPPOSITE TOP: Tim Burton and composer Danny Elfman during work on the film's music.

OPPOSITE BOTTOM: Danny Elfman conducting the orchestra for the film's score.

RIGHT: Composer Danny Elfman.

Alongside the musical numbers, Elfman penned the film's score. He wanted the score cues to echo or hint at the songs, a process that became a jigsaw puzzle for Elfman to solve. "I loved doing the score because it was such a challenge," he explains. "I'd never had something where I was really dealing with so many different thematic elements. But, for me, that's kind of heaven because I love writing in a narrative thematic way. So having so many melodies to work with was just a pleasure . . . I just had so much fun doing that score."

As Elfman was writing, Henry Selick was preparing to shoot the first stop-motion scenes. The director was patiently awaiting demos of the music, so Elfman and Burton went into a recording studio for one very long night where Elfman recorded nearly every vocal part in the film. "Recording the demos, Tim was like the producer, and I was behind the glass in a small recording studio, and we'd just go song by song, laying down all the voices," the songwriter remembers. "At the end of that session we were talking, and I said, 'Look, Tim, I don't know how to put this. But I really need to sing Jack.' And he goes, 'You'll sing the part, don't worry.' Originally, I didn't think of it as for me. But then, as I got into Jack's character, I became so attached to it, I simply found it impossible to give it up."

Once the film was cast, Elfman rerecorded the vocals and the songs with the rest of the actors. As with so much in the film's development, the voice-over work was intrinsically shaped by the cast members involved. In fact, Elfman ended up using several of his own original demo vocals in the final versions for Jack. For the bit parts, like the inhabitants of Halloween Town, he assembled a small group of singers, including Greg Proops and Randy Crenshaw. No one was cast in a particular role; instead, Elfman wanted to improvise everything in the studio. "It was just winging it song by song," he remembers. "It was really fun because it was a very talented group. And in that group, everybody could just switch and swap voices. It was all done in a very improvisational manner of who's doing what. Nothing was planned out going into the vocal sessions. And I knew that any voice that anybody else couldn't do, *I* could, because I'd already done all the character voices on the demos."

THIS SPREAD: Story sketches of Jack in Christmas Town from the musical number "What's This?"

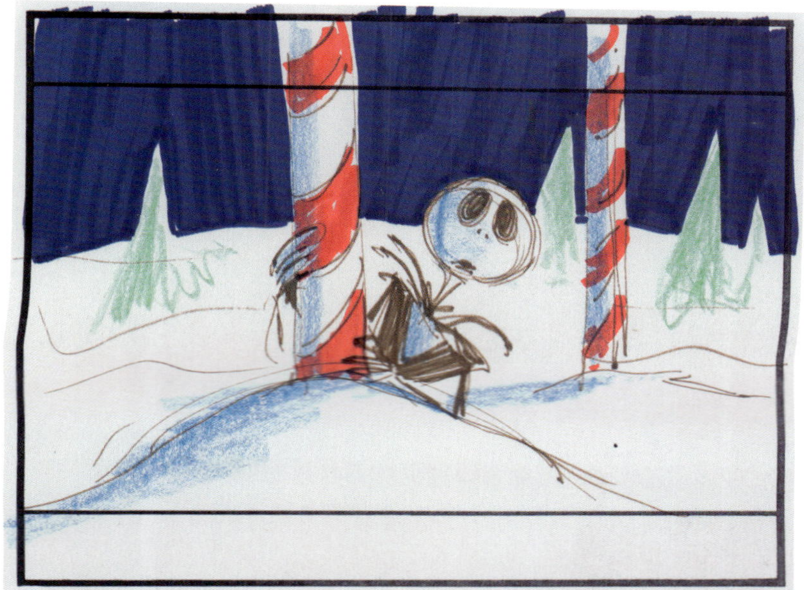

Despite any challenges along the way, writing the music in *Tim Burton's The Nightmare Before Christmas* felt almost effortless for Elfman. He credits Burton for some of the favorite lyrics in the film, including a quip about finding a head in the lake during "Town Meeting Song," as well as the feeling that there were no creative restrictions or boundaries. "The initial creation part was about the simplest thing I've ever done," he recalls. "Over the years, I've had things that were really a struggle and still turn out good and I love them. And there are certain things here and there that just seem to come together quickly, simply, and without effort, and *Nightmare* was one of those. Going through Tim, channeling through me, into these songs."

pan past photos

A SOUND INFLUENCE

Like the film itself, the original soundtrack to *Tim Burton's The Nightmare Before Christmas*, released October 13, 1993, was not a massive mainstream hit. Although Danny Elfman's work was nominated for a Golden Globe for Best Original Score, the album peaked at No. 64 on the *Billboard* Top 200 chart and then quickly lost momentum. The music, despite being one of the film's most memorable aspects, seemed doomed to fall by the cultural wayside as the movie had. However, as *Nightmare* picked up speed years later, thanks to its growing fan base and frequent home video and theatrical rereleases, its songs gained a similarly impassioned following, who have continued to celebrate the beloved tunes.

As the original songs have captivated music fans throughout the years, many reinterpretations have also emerged. To coincide with the film's 2006 rerelease in Disney Digital 3-D, Walt Disney Records unveiled a special edition of the soundtrack featuring a bonus disc with covers by five popular artists: Fall Out Boy, Panic! at the Disco, Fiona Apple, and She Wants Revenge. The special edition release of the film's soundtrack was so successful that two years later, around the film's fifteenth anniversary, the record label decided to create an entire covers album of Elfman's songs, dubbed *Nightmare Revisited*. The album featured twenty total tracks, including both the film's musical numbers and its score cues. Walt Disney Records enlisted a vast range of musicians for the project, from Plain White T's to The Polyphonic Spree to Rise Against.

THIS SPREAD: Jack singing during the "What's This?" sequence—the first song created and animated for the film.

"I wanted to literally reinvent and revisit this whole soundtrack," explains Dani Markman, A&R at Walt Disney Records, who helmed the album alongside Tom MacDougall (who today is the president of Walt Disney Music). "It was fairly daunting because there were quite a few tracks. I wanted it to seem truthful and organic to [*Nightmare*], so it wasn't just about who I was liking at that moment and who was popular—it was really about who was right for the track. I felt like overall *Nightmare Revisited* was going to be a darker release. I really didn't want it to feel like it was pop in any way. What came together, magically, is a perfect amalgam of the best of all of these interesting, remarkable musicians that shared as much passion as I did about this music."

Markman felt that Amy Lee, the singer of rock band Evanescence, was the best possible choice to reimagine "Sally's Song," and that Korn's version of "Kidnap the Sandy Claws," was an inevitable inclusion. But not all the artists were household names, especially those Markman and MacDougall recruited for the instrumental score cues. Icelandic group amiina recorded a new rendition of "Doctor Finkelstein/In the Forest," whereas tribute band Vitamin String Quartet offered their version of "Jack and Sally Montage." The aim was for each artist to personalize a particular song in their own style.

"I gave them full rein," Markman notes. "Tom and I were there for our respective artists to give some feedback, but for the most part, we really didn't need to because the tracks were all pretty great. And we let them hire whoever they wanted. We told them, 'This is what we can afford to give you and all we ask is that you deliver a great track to us.'"

Although participating in *Nightmare Revisited* was an unequivocal yes for everyone involved, the process was not without its hurdles. Many of the artists found it nearly impossible to translate Elfman's musical score into pop or rock music. It was surprising just how complicated the arrangements actually were, which proved intimidating in the recording studio. Chicago punk band Rise Against covered "Making Christmas," a feat so challenging frontman Tim McIlrath says the group has never played the song since they initially recorded it.

REINTERPRETING "SALLY'S SONG"

Like with "Jack's Lament," for "Sally's Song" Elfman drew on classic Hollywood musicals, as well as Kurt Weill and the sound of Berlin in the 1930s. Ultimately, though, the song reflects the heroine herself. "The song was really just inspired by the character in Tim's description of her," Elfman recalls. "It was very simple, and [we] felt that her song should also be very simple, with just the emotions that she was feeling."

For the film, actress Catherine O'Hara sang "Sally's Song," a plaintive ballad that lasts less than two minutes. The scene was animated by Trey Thomas, who drew his inspiration from O'Hara's vocals. "I think that's a beautiful little performance," the animator notes of O'Hara's contribution. "It's this delicate, little, shaky, frail thing that I just loved."

"The song itself is beautiful," O'Hara adds, reflecting on what she wanted to convey. "Sally's concern for Jack's welfare, along with her powerful yearning to be seen by him, is something too many of us know all too well."

Over the years, more and more singers have offered their own versions of "Sally's Song," including Fiona Apple and Amy Lee. "*The Nightmare Before Christmas* is my number one biggest influence artistically in every way," Lee told *SPIN* in 2008. "[When I was young] I literally would sit in my bedroom and sing 'Sally's Song,' or in the car driving to school. The best part about it [recording the song] was that I had no restrictions or direction or anything. I picked the producer, who's a friend, and we just made the song however we wanted together."

For the German version of the film's soundtrack, singer Nina Hagen infused the character's song with an ethereal pop sensibility, whereas a raucous punk rendition by Scott Murphy appeared on the Japanese edition of *Nightmare Revisited*. On October 7, 2013, Helena Bonham Carter embodied Sally for a theatrical rendition of the tune at London's Royal Albert Hall as part of the world premiere of Danny Elfman's Music from the Films of Tim Burton. The actress was accompanied by John Mauceri leading the BBC Concert Orchestra, and the event marked one of the first times Elfman's songs from *Tim Burton's The Nightmare Before Christmas* were showcased during a live event. In the years since, O'Hara has revisited the song, as have Billie Eilish and Phoebe Bridgers, who have both performed as Sally onstage, in Los Angeles in 2021 and London in 2022, respectively.

THIS SPREAD: Sally—voiced by Catherine O'Hara—singing "Sally's Song."

"I don't remember any creative guidelines," McIlrath recalls. "If there were, we ignored them. We got the offer, we jumped on it, and we got a deadline. We were making a record at the time and we were in the studio in Chicago, at a studio called Gravity Studios in Wicker Park. We were so focused on the album that we were thinking, 'This will just be a fun cover song and we'll knock it out.' And I remember us being totally wrong. We started really listening to the song and we realized, 'Holy shit, these arrangements are psychotic. How are we going to make this happen?' We really had to pop the hood on that song. It was one of the more challenging things we've ever had to play or record."

Plain White T's, who covered "Poor Jack," asked the record label for Elfman's musical score sheets to help translate the song for a band. To reimagine the song, bassist Mike Retondo learned all of the score parts on acoustic guitar and bass, and then recorded each part one by one to layer over each other. "It was a weird, weird musical thing that was very much outside of our wheelhouse," he remembers. "It's not a pop song, so for band members slinging electric guitars, it was a big jump."

The final version, which Plain White T's have also never played live, is comprised of Retondo and singer Tom Higgenson, who wanted to bring a sense of theatricality to the cover. "That was a challenge," Higgenson says. "Because the way Jack sings in the movie, the songs are in the key of speech. He's almost talking it and then singing a little bit here and there. We agreed to it thinking, 'Oh, yeah, that'll be awesome.' And then, when it came time to actually do it, we were like, 'What did we sign up for? How are we going to do this?' Luckily, Mike is a really exceptional musician and instrumentalist. He did all the heavy lifting."

Korn frontman Jonathan Davis was a longtime fan of the film when the band was brought on to cover "Kidnap the Sandy Claws," and he had been collecting merchandise for years prior. Although Korn has also never performed the cover since recording it, Davis did join Elfman onstage for a special rendition with the Metropolitan Camerata Orchestra in Mexico City in 2017. That performance exemplified what Davis wanted to bring to the version on *Nightmare Revisited*.

"It was one thing for a band to do a rock cover, but I wanted it to allude to the theater, like being onstage," Davis explains. "That was my intention when singing it, and that's why the way I projected it and the way I did my voice was with a long enunciated, very dramatic delivery. I wanted it to feel like how it felt when you watched the movie—a big theatrical production. Even though it's animated, it just feels like it should be on a stage, belting out to the masses."

Nightmare Revisited peaked at No. 31 on the *Billboard* Top 200 chart, but hit No. 1 on the *Billboard* Top Compilation Albums chart. The success of *Nightmare Revisited* led to Walt Disney Records creating similar compilation albums for future Burton movies *Alice in Wonderland* and *Frankenweenie*. *Almost Alice*, featuring artists like The Cure's Robert Smith and Scottish rock band Franz Ferdinand, came out in 2010, whereas *Frankenweenie Unleashed!*, released in 2012, showcased original songs and covers by the likes of Imagine Dragons, Karen O, and Plain White T's. The record label also compiled *Avengers Assemble*, around 2012's Marvel Studios film *The Avengers*, and *Muppets: The Green Album*, a collection of Muppets-inspired covers, in 2011. It was clear with *Nightmare Revisited* that fans were interested in the various ways classic film songs could be reworked, particularly those that felt too edgy for a mass audience.

Elfman himself has continued to breathe new life into the songs. To celebrate the twenty-fifth anniversary of their partnership, Elfman and Burton released *The Danny Elfman & Tim Burton 25th Anniversary Music Box* in 2010. The expansive collection, which included sixteen CDs and a DVD in a limited-edition zoetrope box, showcased music from *Tim Burton's The Nightmare Before Christmas*, as well as films like *Edward Scissorhands*, *Batman*, and *Sleepy Hollow*. Warner Bros sold an exclusive limited number of one thousand box sets in total, making it a highly sought-after collectible.

The CDs featured the songs and scores known and loved by the fans, but the most exciting inclusion was the unheard tracks and demos Elfman created while writing for *Nightmare*. An unused song from the film, "This Time," sung by Elfman, emerged alongside rough demos. Pulling the box set together was a massive task for Elfman's agents Richard Kraft and Laura Engel, largely because Elfman hadn't catalogued any of his material. In fact, Kraft ended up searching through garbage bags full of cassette tapes in Elfman's garage to compile the tracks for the box set.

"We dug up archival stuff from *The Nightmare Before Christmas*—a lot of Danny's original demos and a lot of underscore that was never on the soundtrack," Kraft recalls. "It was such a nerd spectacular. For instance, in 'What's This?' there's a moment where some elves cross the screen and sing 'La, la, la, la' as a counterpoint. I read message boards of nerds and they were always complaining that the elf choir was not included on the original soundtrack. So, I went and found that track and added it to the background of the song. Finally, the elves could be heard."

Contemporary artists continue to cover the songs from *Tim Burton's The Nightmare Before Christmas*. In 2020, Disney's official a cappella group DCappella released "The Nightmare Before Christmas Medley" to celebrate Halloween, which for DCapella member Joe Santoni, was an opportunity to pay tribute to Elfman's work by giving it a new spin, "This movie and Danny Elfman's unforgettable soundtrack has always been one of my favorites [and] I hope that when people hear our arrangement, they hear something new and different, but that we still managed to capture the wonderfully strange and peculiar elements of Elfman's original soundtrack." The following Halloween, in 2021, indie rock duo Larkin Poe showcased an instrumental cover of "Sally's Song" performed on slide guitar, and later that year Matt Heafy, lead singer of metal band Trivium, dropped a heavy, electric-guitar driven rendition of "Jack's Lament."

In 2003, fans buzzed with excitement as blink-182 sang about Jack and Sally's enduring love in the emo-tinged single "I Miss You," which appeared on the band's fifth studio album, *blink-182*. Cowritten by guitarist Tom DeLonge and bassist Mark Hoppus and produced by Jerry Finn, the acoustic song was inspired by The Cure's 1983 track "The Love Cats," as well as *Tim Burton's The Nightmare Before Christmas*. It was officially released as a single on February 2, 2004, just in time for Valentine's Day, and went on to be certified gold. According to Hoppus, it was drummer Travis Barker's idea to include the Jack and Sally reference in "I Miss You." "We were writing a song with dark lyrics about love," he remembers, "and Travis said, 'What about *The Nightmare Before Christmas?*' For our generation, *Nightmare* was such a huge movie not only in its aesthetic, but in its themes, its production design, and music."

Although the song's music video, directed by Jonas Auckerland, doesn't directly reference the film, it is set in a haunted manor, with shots of a graveyard and supernatural elements. The band filmed the video in an old mansion overlooking Hollywood with the intention of creating something "Gothic and dark and weird." In the years since its release, the song has been covered by numerous artists, including 5 Seconds of Summer, and inspired The Chainsmokers' 2016 single "Closer." It marked a turning point for blink-182, as well as a key touchpoint for fans of Jack and Sally.

"'I Miss You' is an important song for blink-182 because it was such a departure from anything we had done prior to that point," Hoppus says. "We wrote it in a rented house in Rancho Santa Fe on acoustic guitars, and it came together in a very special, magical way. It's one of the highlights of the album."

OPPOSITE: Jack sings to Sally atop Spiral Hill in their final duet.

BOTTOM: Sally hidden during the "Jack's Lament" sequence.

LIVE PERFORMANCES

The energetic theatricality of the music in *Tim Burton's The Nightmare Before Christmas* allows the songs to translate seamlessly to a live performance. In fact, the first time Danny Elfman performed a song from the film onstage was prior to its release, at an exhibition for movie theater owners in Las Vegas. Elfman sang a rendition of "What's This?" for the crowd, who gathered in the summer of 1993 to learn about upcoming releases. The musician received a perplexed reaction. "I would describe the reaction as a bit like staring into the eye of a chicken," recalls Richard Kraft, Elfman's comanager and agent who has also produced many of the live *Nightmare* shows. "It was perfect that the song was called 'What's This?' because the exhibitors were asking themselves the same question. In no way did it give me any peace of mind that things were going to go well."

"I was so nervous I blacked it out of my memory," Elfman says of the performance. "I sang to a track, and I think it went horribly. Technically, I was performing it live, but it wasn't like performing it onstage."

After the film came out, Elfman left his band, Oingo Boingo, who played their final show at the Universal Amphitheatre on Halloween night in 1995. Once the band had said farewell, Elfman moved on to score films like *Mission: Impossible* (1996), *Good Will Hunting* (1997), and Burton's *Sleepy Hollow* (1999). He didn't return to the stage as a singer, though he continued to appear at various live events in support of *Tim Burton's The Nightmare Before Christmas*. Two decades after the movie's release, things changed unexpectedly for the musician, who rediscovered his love for performing live thanks to his ongoing collaboration with Burton.

As another celebration of their decades long collaboration, Elfman and Burton put together a concert at Royal Albert Hall in London on October 7, 2013. Initially, it was intended as an instrumental symphony performance conducted by John Mauceri, but late in the planning process, Kraft convinced Elfman to go onstage as Jack. "We got the booking, and there was no show," Kraft remembers, "so there was a mad scramble to put together an evening of music from their collaboration." He also recalls that his suggestion to have the concert culminate with Elfman singing some songs from *Nightmare* had "presented an interesting quandary."

"At that point, it was almost eighteen years since I'd sung publicly," Elfman explains. "That's a big break. I didn't know if I could do it. I had a lot of stage fright my whole life—it actually never got better. When I retired from performing in '95, I didn't miss it. Even though I missed the energy of the shows, I didn't miss the hell I went through psychologically walking out onstage in front of an audience, which was incredibly difficult for me."

That night, standing backstage at Royal Albert Hall, Elfman froze. But in the wings behind him was Helena Bonham Carter, preparing to sing "Sally's Song." The actress encouraged Elfman out onto the stage and, in that moment, his career once again changed completely. "It was really one of the big emotional experiences of my life," he recalls, "because I really had to push past this wall and go out there. I had absolutely no idea what to expect. I was prepared for the worst, but I was astonished by the wonderful, warm response. It was a great experience doing Jack live for the first time. To this day, that performance—doing Jack live—was, and still is, one of the greatest nights of my life."

The response was so strong and the concert so lauded that Elfman and Kraft began to consider the idea of doing an entire live concert of *Tim Burton's The Nightmare Before Christmas*. To test it, Elfman first brought a production to Tokyo in 2015 and performed most of the vocals himself. It was immediately successful, which led the team to discuss where to bring the show next. "We were at a restaurant in Tokyo and Danny said, 'That was interesting. Why don't we do it at the Hollywood Bowl?'" Kraft recounts. "And we said, 'Great, that gives us a year and a half to get it together,' because it was something we wanted to do around Halloween. And he said, 'No, I meant this year.'"

"*The Nightmare Before Christmas* Live at the Hollywood Bowl" debuted on Halloween night in 2015. Elfman returned to voice Jack, with an orchestra again conducted by Mauceri. Ken Page and Catherine O'Hara reprised their film roles of Oogie Boogie and Sally, and Paul Reubens made a surprise appearance for a rendition of Lock,

OPPOSITE: Composer Danny Elfman performs during the concert, "Danny Elfman's Music from the Films of Tim Burton" in Prague, Czech Republic, March 25, 2014.

Shock, and Barrel's "Kidnap the Sandy Claws." Elfman concluded the evening with a performance of Oingo Boingo's "Dead Man's Party" with his former bandmate Steve Bartek.

Since then, "*The Nightmare Before Christmas* Live at the Hollywood Bowl" has returned several times, in 2016, 2018, 2019, and 2023. The cast has reprised their roles at subsequent shows, some of which have featured live projections by creative studio Mousetrappe on the iconic arch of the Hollywood Bowl. Each performance has been bigger and more elaborate—and every show has sold out. For the cast members, the performances have revealed how expansive the fan base of *Tim Burton's The Nightmare Before Christmas* has truly become.

"That's when I really began to understand the following for the film and the whole experience of it," said Page. "Because until you see everybody in one place, you go, 'Yeah, okay, people like it.' The concerts are where you really understand not only the fan base, but also the art form that the film really is projecting on these huge screens. And it's a very unique experience because people not only get to see us live in front of them, but they also see the technical art form of doing voice-over work for a film. I've been floored by the reaction that I get."

"It's really exciting," Reubens said. "I felt like the audience was really excited I was there and they loved the music and they loved the movie and you could feel that. It has practically become a yearly thing and is really fun."

For O'Hara, returning to the stage as Sally has been nerve-wracking, but also very rewarding. "It has been really exciting to sing a beautiful song with a beautiful orchestra in front of thousands of people who just want me to be Sally," the actress says. "I was scared before each performance because I hadn't sung the song for over twenty years and I was expected to sing it in the original key. I had a few voice lessons and practiced a lot at home. It's a very tricky song to sing, though the final effect needs to feel pure and simple. It really helped that the movie was playing behind me on the big screen and I hoped the audience was focused on that real Sally while I sang."

BELOW: Danny Elfman performing at the 2023 Hollywood Bowl concert in Los Angeles, California.

In 2020, after the COVID-19 pandemic made live performances an impossibility, several Broadway actors came together for a virtual benefit concert of the film's music in partnership with Elfman, Burton, and Disney Music Group. The one-night event, held on Halloween, was live-streamed for audiences around the world. It was directed by actor James Monroe Iglehart, who also performed as Oogie Boogie, and featured Rafael Casal as Jack, Adrienne Warren as Sally, Nik Walker as Lock, Lesli Margherita as Shock, Rob McClure as Barrel, and Danny Burstein as the narrator. Proceeds from the concert benefited the Lymphoma Research Foundation and The Actors Fund, which supported out-of-work stage actors during the pandemic shutdown.

As the world began to reopen in 2021, Elfman and Kraft wanted to devise a way to bring *Tim Burton's The Nightmare Before Christmas* back to the stage. For two nights, over Halloween weekend, *Tim Burton's The Nightmare Before Christmas* Live-To-Film Concert took over the Banc of California Stadium in Los Angeles. O'Hara was unavailable due to her filming schedule, so the team invited Billie Eilish to stand in as Sally and "Weird Al" Yankovic to perform as Shock. Elfman, Page, and Reubens voiced their onscreen roles, with Page receiving the biggest standing ovation of the evening when he came out as Oogie Boogie. To create a more immersive experience, Kraft brought in a sixteen-foot-tall Jack Skellington puppet that was originally made for the Disney Parks. Elfman wrote new narration for Jack, which was recorded and programmed for the puppet, who emerged repeatedly throughout the concert.

Elfman has continued to showcase the film's music outside the United States as well. The musician held a series of three concerts, *The Nightmare Before Christmas* Live in Tokyo, at the Tokyo International Forum in the spring of 2019, and later that year *Tim Burton's The Nightmare Before Christmas* Live in Concert came to London's OVO Arena Wembley for two nights in December. Page and O'Hara, as well as Mauceri, flew to England to perform at the events. Elfman returned to the London venue in December of 2022 for a rendition of *Nightmare*'s songs synced to the film, accompanied by the BBC Concert Orchestra and joined by Phoebe Bridgers as Sally and original cast member Ken Page. In December 2024, he performed at the OVO Arena Wembley again, this time with the Spice Girls' Emma Bunton (aka Baby Spice). Although most of the live events have involved a screening of the film projected behind the musical performance, Danny Elfman has toyed with other formats. In the spring of 2022, he took the stage at the popular Coachella Valley Music and Arts Festival, performing a showcase of his musical career. Initially booked as part of the festival's lineup in 2020, the performance was delayed for two years due to the pandemic, allowing Elfman and his team more time to conceptualize the best possible sixty-minute set. The set included an array of the songwriter's film contributions, as well as songs from Oingo Boingo and his 2021 solo studio album, *Big Mess*. To celebrate *Tim Burton's The Nightmare Before Christmas*, Elfman created a new mash-up of "Jack's Lament," "This Is Halloween," and "What's This?" The reaction from fans and the press was immense. Between the first and second weekend of the festival, Elfman's audience multiplied significantly thanks to word of mouth and social media.

For Elfman, these live performances affirm the legacy of *Nightmare*. The ongoing enthusiastic response helps ease the initial pain he felt when the film disappeared after its theatrical release. The film and its music were revived beyond anyone's wildest dreams.

"Of everything I'd worked on at that point, if I could pick the one thing that I could wish a second life on, it was *Nightmare*," Elfman reflects. "Because I've worked on plenty of movies that failed. Probably the majority. But on very rare occasions, there are films that don't do that well but then maintain the life on their own afterwards. If you would have told me I'd be doing *Nightmare* live onstage and I'd have sold out eight shows at the Hollywood Bowl, I would have said you were insane. But here we are."

CHAPTER 9

A COLLECTOR'S *NIGHTMARE*: MERCHANDISE, GAMES, AND ODDITIES

"I think the demand [for *Nightmare*] was always there, and we were the ones catching up."

— TERRELL GENTRY, SENIOR MANAGER OF DESIGN AT DISNEY PARKS, EXPERIENCES AND PRODUCTS

Over time, *Tim Burton's The Nightmare Before Christmas* has become so ubiquitous in pop culture that it can seem almost impossible to go a day without seeing Jack Skellington's face. The dapper king of Halloween is emblazoned on T-shirts and hats, printed onto yoga leggings, and even found on infant onesies. He's a daily inspiration in the lives of many fans, both in their homes as toys and décor and on their bodies as fashion. Although themed merchandise has been available since *Nightmare* opened in theaters in 1993, the volume and variety have increased year by year. In fact, it continues to grow in a way that is almost unparalleled in Hollywood. It's fair to say that a portion of *Nightmare*'s success is due to this constant surge of product, all of which is seen and sanctioned by Tim Burton's team before it hits stores.

"Merchandising has arguably been as crucial to the success of *The Nightmare Before Christmas* as it has been to *Star Wars*," explains Lisa Morton, author of *Trick or Treat: A History of Halloween*. "*Nightmare* benefited from the power of a marketing behemoth behind it, and they took advantage of it early on, although it increased exponentially over the years. I'm astonished at seeing ads now for things like *Nightmare* cuckoo clocks. The film's original release in 1993 also coincided with the rise of Halloween collectibles, so it provided a new tsunami of delightful collectibles that were more affordable than many of the sought-after vintage pieces."

'TIS THE SEASON ALL YEAR-ROUND

Initially, the merchandise available for fans of *Tim Burton's The Nightmare Before Christmas* was relatively limited. Though it was possible for fans of the film to bring the characters home after seeing *Nightmare* in theaters, there simply wasn't enough product available in stores. "*Nightmare*'s merchandising remains one of the few cases in which initial demand actually exceeded the amount of material available," Morton noted in her book. In fact, Disney wasn't sure what the best strategy was to market *Nightmare* toys.

"It was really hit-or-miss, that first wave of merchandise," says director Henry Selick. "There was not a whole lot. It was like, 'What's the game plan here?'"

As *Tim Burton's The Nightmare Before Christmas* has grown in popularity, so has the amount of merchandise. The strategy behind the scenes at Disney Parks, Experiences and Products, which licenses the film to various retailers, is fan-first. As there is more demand from the fans, more items become available. Since the late 2010s, the film has transitioned from a niche brand sold in fan-centric shops like Hot Topic to a brand supported by mass retailers like Walmart. The film's merchandising shifted from a seasonal business, centered around Halloween and Christmas, to being a year-round property. Today, the products are intended to serve both the core audience, who have followed *Nightmare* since its inception, and those who have joined the Halloween Town crew more recently.

"People want it all," says Elise Barkan, former Director of Global Franchise Development & Marketing at Disney Parks, Experiences and Products. Barkan adds that the goal is to create

PAGE 150: Jack emerges from the toxic green fountain and hailed as the Pumpkin King of Halloween Town.

TOP: Early sketches of Jack and Sally.

OPPOSITE: Concept art of Jack Skellington by assistant art director Kelly Asbury.

merchandise and consumer experiences that embrace the film's aesthetic and themes. Burton's original drawings remain at the core of every piece of apparel, toy, and collectible because that visual storytelling is what makes the merchandise so memorable. "The artistry in Tim Burton's work, and this film in particular, was disruptive," she explains. "And there's something about positive disruption that sticks with people. The story is unexpected—it turns everything on its ear. It just lets people's imaginations flourish. It's like, 'Oh, I never thought about Halloween and Christmas this way.'"

Although Jack Skellington has always been the visual signifier of *Tim Burton's The Nightmare Before Christmas*, over the years Sally has become just as popular with consumers. Nowadays, fans can find most of the film's characters and sets—and even small details like the beloved Deadly Nightshade jar—as the inspiration for toys, games, clothing, and more. Ultimately, though, Jack and Sally remain the fan favorites.

"It's the eternal love story," says Terrell Gentry, Senior Manager, Product Design at Disney Parks, Experiences and Products. "I've worked on a lot of products for various franchises, and usually you have the main hero who is very popular, but I would say consumers really like Jack and Sally equally. We create a lot of items of Sally by herself, a lot of items with Jack by himself, and a lot of products with them together. The only other set of characters I could put on that same level would be Mickey and Minnie."

For Burton, it's miraculous to see Jack's face everywhere he goes. "I see Jack almost every day," Burton says. "It's incredible. That's the most shocking thing, but it makes me feel better than almost anything. It's a connection that I just feel very emotional and amazed about."

TOYS, COLLECTIBLES, AND DÉCOR

BELOW: Jack Skellington puppet with his numerous replacement heads to accommodate any expression.

OPPOSITE TOP: An idea for a LEGO set featuring the Spiral Hill and parts of Halloween Town.

OPPOSITE BOTTOM LEFT: *Nightmare* merchandise comes in all forms, including this Jack Skellington slow cooker.

OPPOSITE BOTTOM RIGHT: Funko Pop! vinyl of Jack and Sally on the Spiral Hill.

From the very beginning, the goal was to capture the visual aesthetic and thematic essence of the film and its characters in any toys, dolls, or other merchandise without compromising Burton's original vision. A Jack doll needed to evoke the Jack that audiences saw on the screen, even if he was not an exact replica. Similarly, a mug or T-shirt should feel true to the film itself, acting as an extension of the story and the world.

Visual consultant Rick Heinrichs, who hired several of the film's crew to help create the so-called "Design Bible," spent a lot of time finessing the concept art to ensure any toys or action figures would be of the best possible quality. Jack, with his long, thin limbs, was the most difficult character to translate from the screen into a consumer product. Despite these challenges, Heinrichs endeavored to keep a connection between products and the film itself through the style guide—a sensibility and goal that continues to drive the design and creation of toys themed around *Tim Burton's The Nightmare Before Christmas*.

In late 1993, available products included T-shirts, mugs, buttons, Christmas ornaments, dolls, and stationery. A popular collectible, sold by Disney Art Editions and signed by Burton, was "The 12 Faces of Jack," which featured twelve Jack Skellington heads with different facial expressions. Only 275 were created in total and the item has since become a coveted piece, with sets selling for thousands of dollars in online auctions in recent years. The primary items that hit store shelves were action figures by Hasbro, whose run included the Werewolf (as he was credited on the packaging), Behemoth, the Mayor, a glow-in-the-dark Oogie Boogie, Santa Claus, the Evil Scientist (as labeled on the packaging), Sally, two versions of Jack Skellington—as the Pumpkin King and dressed as Santa—and a trio set of Lock, Shock, and Barrel. Each was packaged with a custom accessory, including a purse for Sally and a megaphone for the Mayor. Hasbro also released larger sixteen-inch Jack and Sally dolls, a Santa Claus hand puppet, and an Oogie Boogie plush doll filled with "bugs."

One of the only *Nightmare* branded tie-ins in the fall of 1993 was a collection of colorful, plastic watches that were part of a Burger King promotion. The watches were available for a mere $1.99 along with the purchase of a value meal at the fast-food franchises. Fans were encouraged to collect all four, which were emblazoned with images of the characters and scenes from Halloween Town and Christmas Town. The watches now sell as collectibles online, going for more money as a four-piece set with the original boxes.

ABOVE: Wearable masks of Jack and Sally from Funko Pop!

OPPOSITE: *Tim Burton's The Nightmare Before Christmas Tarot Deck and Guidebook* with sample cards.

Indeed, as the film began to acquire a bigger fan base, the demand for toys and merchandise grew as well. By the late 1990s, as the film grew in popularity thanks to home video and DVD sales, Disney began to respond to the desire for more products.

Terrell Gentry, who helped create the expanded style guide, said "By the late '90s, that [increased] demand was definitely there. That might have actually spurred a bit more interest in the film . . . [which] spurred on things like the overlay at Disneyland, which created more demand. The opportunity just seems to keep growing."

Today, Burton credits Japanese toy companies with infusing new life into the merchandise created for *Tim Burton's The Nightmare Before Christmas*. Japan was hungry for products after the film came out in theaters there in the fall of 1994, and Japanese doll company JUN Planning Co., Inc.—now based in South Korea and operating under the name Groove—created numerous lines of *Nightmare* action figures, figurines, and dolls beginning in the late 1990s. Several of the dolls, including limited-edition variations on Jack Skellington, arrived in coffin-shaped boxes. A "Gold Millennium Edition," released in the year 2000 with a limited run of 2,000, is one of the most striking: Jack's body, head, and clothing are coated in gold as he resides in a gold coffin. JUN Planning Co., Inc.'s figures are notably detailed, often including accessories for the characters. In 2004, for the tenth anniversary of the film in Japan, the company designed a set with Lock, Shock, and Barrel riding in their bathtub, as well as a Jack figure who came with an angry face and a chair. "I think it struck a chord in Japan particularly," remembers Heinrichs. "There was a lot of interest and appetite for the merch from their side—and some pretty cool clothing and toys came out of their exploration of our graphic language, as well."

Action figures based on the movie continued to be extremely popular, particularly as these new designs emerged. In 2002, collectible merchandising company NECA unveiled several *Nightmare* marionettes, followed by four life-size plush dolls of Jack and Sally in 2003 and between 2004 to 2007, and nearly every character in the film.

Disney
Tim Burton's
The Nightmare Before Christmas
Tarot Deck
and Guidebook

ACE OF POTIONS

XV THE DEVIL

XIX THE SUN

VI THE LOVERS

THE FOOL

XIV TEMPERANCE

ACE OF POTIONS

XIX THE SUN

THE FOOL

XV THE DEVIL

VI THE LOVERS

XIV TEMPERANCE

CHRISTMAS ORNAMENTS AND FESTIVE CURIOSITIES

Throughout the years, the world of *Tim Burton's The Nightmare Before Christmas* has brought a sense of festive cheer to fans around Christmas time. Through Christmas tree ornaments, holiday decorations, and even advent calendars, Jack and his crew help liven up every home.

LEFT: Blow-up décor of the Clown with the Tear-away Face.

OPPOSITE: *Nightmare* merchandise featuring Lock, Shock, and Barrel.

Sometimes, the storytelling in products is less about replicating something from the film directly and more about using the characters or the aesthetic as a point of reference. One example of that is the 2018 series of *Tim Burton's The Nightmare Before Christmas* Hot Wheels cars, which interpreted the film's characters as existing Hot Wheels vehicles. The brand continues to sell themed cars and even created a short stop-motion film with the Jack and Sally cars for the holidays in 2021. In 2015, artist Jasmine Becket-Griffith designed a collection of fairy figurines inspired by *Nightmare*, sold via the Hamilton Collection. Becket-Griffith imagined her signature fairies holding *Nightmare* dolls, including Jack, Sally, Oogie Boogie, and Zero, which were sold with a Halloween Town display. More recently, Hot Topic began selling a Jack Skellington cheese board, a black-and-white *Nightmare* slow cooker, and a wooden serving plank emblazoned with the phase "Now and forever." Funko has also joined in the excitement of revisiting the inhabitants of Halloween Town in a variety of ways, including in an advent calendar and as glow-in-the-dark figures.

Tim Burton's The Nightmare Before Christmas continues to be reimagined in creative, compelling ways, often from unexpected brands or retailers. Jack and Sally were crafted into a LEGO Brickheadz set for the film's twenty-fifth anniversary, and in 2019, the characters appeared in a LEGO minifigures set. In 2022, UK-based LEGO builder Simon Scott created his own ambitious take on Halloween Town using existing figures and pieces, as no official *Nightmare* LEGO set had yet existed. Scott submitted his grand design to LEGO Ideas, a program in which builders can gain support for their designs and potentially have them reviewed by the company. The following year, LEGO approved it for production. The result was LEGO's first full-fledged *Tim Burton's The Nightmare Before Christmas* set, released in September 2024. Featuring nearly 2,200 pieces, eight key characters from the film, and iconic locations like Spiral Hill, Halloween Town Hall, and Jack's house, the set instantly connected with its audience.

VIDEO GAMES AND BOARD GAMES

Although *Tim Burton's The Nightmare Before Christmas* is full of memorable visuals and exciting adventures, it took some time for games to be developed based on the original world of the film. Throughout the past few decades, both board games and video games themed to match the movie have appeared in stores, and the 2002 release of *Kingdom Hearts* marked the first time that characters from *Nightmare* appeared in a video game. The action role-playing game featured a protagonist who teamed up with Disney characters to fight a group of villains called the Heartless. Gameplay included visits to Halloween Town and Christmas Town, and *Nightmare* characters such as Jack Skellington, Dr. Finkelstein, Oogie Boogie, Sally and Zero. Since then, Jack Skellington and his pals have continued to appear in the Kingdom Hearts series in various iterations.

Meanwhile, thanks to the immense popularity of the film in Japan, game company Capcom began developing a standalone video game for consoles titled *Tim Burton's The Nightmare Before Christmas: Oogie's Revenge* (2004). It follows the events of the film, with Lock, Shock, and Barrel resurrecting Oogie Boogie when Jack leaves town to seek out new ideas for Halloween. Upon Jack's return, the Pumpkin King discovers he needs to save Halloween Town—and Sally—from Oogie Boogie yet again. In 2005, Game Boy Advance unveiled *Tim Burton's The Nightmare Before Christmas: The Pumpkin King*, preceding the events of the film. Also originally developed in Japan, by Tose, the platform game centered on Jack Skellington's first encounter with Oogie Boogie, who desires to turn Halloween into Crawloween. The action sees Jack rescuing Sally for the first time, resulting in their initial meeting, and he defeats Oogie Boogie, who declares he will get his revenge.

"*The Nightmare Before Christmas* really resonates with the gaming audience," explains Sonoko Ishioka, Executive Director for Walt Disney Games. "The characters fit really well in

TOP: The *Tim Burton's The Nightmare Before Christmas* edition of Hasbro's Monopoly.

OPPOSITE: Gameloft's a *Disney Magic Kingdoms*, 2016 city-building game featuring Jack and Sally.

different contexts. We can do something playful and funny, or we can do something more serious and action-oriented. We always think about, 'What is the version of Jack that appears in this world with all these characters?' We think about what his essence is, what his traits are, and then translate that in terms of both gameplay and art style."

In December 2021, popular video game *Fall Guys: Ultimate Knockout* launched a limited-edition collection of *Tim Burton's The Nightmare Before Christmas* character costumes. Players could use points to acquire The Mayor of Halloween Town, Sally, and Jack Skellington, and to play event challenges featuring Santa Jack and Zero. Jack and Oogie Boogie also joined the fun in *Disney Mirrorverse*, a mobile action RPG game released in June of 2022. In the game, alternate-reality versions of the characters could team up with other powerfully amplified versions of Disney heroes and villains to protect the Mirrorverse from the threat of an enemy called the Fractured. And there are no signs of "game over" for the *Nightmare* characters—between 2023 and 2024, they made their way onto popular platform adventures such as *Disney Dreamlight Valley*, *Disney Speedstorm*, the mobile game *Disney Twisted-Wonderland*, and the global gaming phenomenon *Fortnite*.

For players who prefer a more tactile experience, board games continue to be a hit with fans of the film. Themed versions of games like Yahtzee—which uses Jack's head to shake the dice—have been particularly popular over the past decade. One of the first board games, released by NECA in 2004, was an original game titled *Tim Burton's The Nightmare Before Christmas* Game. Players were tasked with kidnapping Sandy Claws and defeating Oogie Boogie—much like the film itself. Now a collectible, the game featured six metal game pieces: Jack, Sally, Dr. Finkelstein, Lock, Shock, and Barrel.

Later, a chess set released for the twenty-fifth anniversary featured Jack as the king of the white game pieces and Oogie Boogie as the king of the black game pieces. Oogie Boogie is also the subject of a themed edition of Operation, in which players are tasked with removing items from the villain's body without setting off the buzzer. There are also *Tim Burton's The Nightmare Before Christmas* versions of Monopoly, Clue, Something Wild!, Trivial Pursuit, Jenga, and Scrabble, as well as puzzles, playing cards, and dice. For many, actively participating in a game allows fans to immerse themselves in the film's story and continue to keep it alive.

FASHION AND STYLE

For a fan of *Tim Burton's The Nightmare Before Christmas*, a Jack Skellington T-shirt is the ultimate fashion statement, but it's not the only sartorial way fans can express their love of the film. In fact, *Nightmare*-themed fashion dates back to before the movie's arrival. In October 1993, as *Tim Burton's The Nightmare Before Christmas* was arriving in theaters, Macy's department store in New York City installed temporary window displays themed to the film. The displays featured small sets from the movie inhabited by characters like Oogie Boogie and props like a headless doll.

Despite the spotlight on the film in a major shopping destination, early apparel options were limited—as with the toys and merchandise. For the most part, *Nightmare* clothing items sold in 1993 were T-shirts featuring Jack Skellington. There was a memorable Bone Daddy T-shirt, featuring Jack posing in front of a sepia-toned background, as well as several shirts with artwork and lettering from the film, including one depicting Jack on Spiral Hill. However, some of what is sold online and in secondhand shops today as "vintage" *Nightmare* apparel may have been fan-made due to the lack of variation in stores.

As with the toys, the fashion options have grown significantly. A major player in that growth has been retailer Hot Topic, which has hundreds of stores throughout the United States, as well as a strong online presence. Early on, Hot Topic sold *Nightmare* T-shirts, Jack Skellington beanies, and accessories alongside toys and collectibles. A favorite item, which continues to be rereleased in a new form each year, was the Bone Daddy cologne and Rag Doll perfume. By the 2000s, the retailer added additional products tied to *Tim Burton's The Nightmare Before Christmas*, including homeware, car accessories, and beauty products. As the film's popularity endures, Hot Topic adapts its themed apparel to contemporary fashion trends. Sally dresses are redesigned each year to reflect what consumers, especially in the demographic of late

LEFT: Apparel inspired by *Tim Burton's The Nightmare Before Christmas* and other Disney films.

OPPOSITE: Merchandise including home goods and apparel have grown increasingly popular in the thirty years since *Nightmare's* release.

teens and early twenties, are wearing. Because *Tim Burton's The Nightmare Before Christmas* merchandise and apparel now saturates the marketplace, retailers like Hot Topic keep pushing the envelope while staying true to Burton's vision.

The interest from consumers has evolved as the film has embedded itself more fully in pop culture. Jack and Sally remain very popular, but more and more merchandise is inspired by Oogie Boogie, including makeup palettes. *Nightmare* is consistently in the top ten franchises sold at Hot Topic, particularly during the fall and holiday seasons. "Even with changing trends, *Nightmare* will still find its voice and be a major property for us in the back half of the year," says Ed LaBay, Executive Vice President, General Merchandise Manager, Marketing, Licensing, and Product Development, who oversees the buyers and marketing for the retailer. "Regardless of the trend cycle between genres and pop culture, *Nightmare* always has a home."

Over the past decade, fashion collaborations have become increasingly popular with fans of *Tim Burton's The Nightmare Before Christmas*, with more brands jumping onboard. For the holidays in 2013, adidas released a glow-in-the-dark, *Nightmare*-themed special edition of Kobe Bryant's retro Crazy 8 silhouette basketball shoe. In October 2019, Vans unveiled a special collection inspired by *Nightmare*, which featured ten pieces of footwear along with various apparel and accessory items. The highlight of the collection was a pair of Sk8-Hi shoes depicting "Jack's Lament," with four panels showcasing frames from Jack's walk through the Halloween Town cemetery. Oogie Boogie, Sally, and Lock, Shock, and Barrel were also spotlighted on various styles, from high-top sneakers to slip-ons. Rather than simply inserting artwork from the film directly onto the shoes, the designers aimed to make something more creative that engaged fans in a more nuanced, clever way.

More recent areas of merchandise that are proving increasingly popular are apparel for children, infants, and pets. While the primary age range for *Nightmare* fashion is eighteen to thirty-five, Disney introduced kids' products in the late 2010s and added on an infant selection in the early 2020s. "There was so much demand in those categories that we opened it up because the fan was really adamant about getting this for their kids," Javier Garcia, senior manager of product design at Disney Parks, Experiences and Products, says, "Now, it's a full family statement."

HALLOWEEN COSTUMES AND MAKEUP

Whereas some fans are content with having *Tim Burton's The Nightmare Before Christmas* characters in toy form, others want to actually become them. Every year, Jack and Sally costumes and face paint fill the shelves of countless Halloween stores, encouraging whole families to transform into Halloween Town's finest. The enduring popularity of *Nightmare* costumes is truly remarkable, inspiring each new generation of trick-or-treaters.

Interestingly, before *Nightmare* was even completed, artistic coordinator Allison Abbate created the first-ever Sally Halloween costume. The film's crew, comprised of artistic, creative people, hosted Halloween parties in which everyone dressed up in their own handmade costumes. For one such occasion, Abbate drew stitches across her face and donned a costume that evoked Sally's final look in the movie.

"I saw a sketch for the sculpt, so I used dresses that I had and then crafted them together into the shape," Abbate remembers. "We hadn't created the puppet yet, so no one knew the character, and I don't even know if Sally had a costume yet. I didn't have the right patterns or fabric, so I did my own interpretation. It was definitely a very DIY costume. But one of the great things about working in stop-motion is that everyone's so talented, and so our Halloween parties were truly the stuff of legend. The creativity and craftsmanship the artists showcased were amazing. People would go all out, so I always felt like I needed to really do it up right to compete."

Abbate may have been the first to dress up as a character from the film, but she is by no means the last. Adults and children alike continue to don *Nightmare* Halloween costumes every year—some enthusiasts wear from Disney's official line, whereas others inspired by the movie prefer crafting their own take on a favorite character. Some *Nightmare* characters have attributes that are quite tricky to depict, like the Mayor's two faces, Dr. Finkelstein's clamshell skull, and Oogie Boogie's bug-filled interior, but this has led to some of the wildest costumes. Of course, *Nightmare* cosplayers are a staple at San Diego Comic-Con, Disney's D23, and other conventions every year. Many have produced unique variations of Jack and Sally, including steampunk versions, a gender-swapped Jack and Sally, and the couple reimagined as anime characters.

For fans who want to transform themselves through professional makeup, creators on YouTube, Instagram, and TikTok have dedicated channels to *Nightmare*-specific makeup tutorials. Even cosmetic companies like ColourPop, Revolution Beauty, and Melt Cosmetics have all released *Tim Burton's The Nightmare Before Christmas* makeup lines with eyeshadow palettes, lipsticks, and beauty tools inspired by the world of Halloween Town.

OPPOSITE: There have been many *Nightmare*-inspired makeup collections over the years—including this collection from Colourpop Cosmetics—which often feature vibrant colors and fun packaging.

Disney
Tim Burton's
The Nightmare Before Christmas
ColourPop
Pressed Powder Palette
Zero
Meant to Be
Dear Friend
In My Bones
Pumpkin Patch
Christmas Town
Frog's Breath
Dr. Finkelstein
What's This
Sandy Claws
Everybody Scream
Halloween Town

CHAPTER 10

REPRISE

"It was sad to say goodbye, but now it never leaves!"
—HENRY SELICK

When production of *Tim Burton's The Nightmare Before Christmas* wrapped in 1993, the crew at Skellington Productions were sorry to have to move on. The film had been a huge piece of their lives for years, and at first, they thought all they'd have to keep were memories. Over the years, however, Jack, Sally, and even Behemoth have stuck around in the cultural imagination, and the crew's involvement in the film has continued. In fact, more than three decades after its release, *Nightmare* continues to gain momentum and reach new audiences in a variety of ways. In 2023, Danny Elfman's catchy tune "This is Halloween" debuted at number forty-one on the *Billboard* Hot 100 chart, despite never having made the chart in its thirty-plus-year existence. By November of that year, the full soundtrack had also spent fifty-nine weeks on the *Billboard* Soundtracks chart.

There is no reason to doubt that this perennial holiday classic will be haunting its fans for many years to come. Its handmade artistry stands out, both against computer-generated animation and against the general landscape of Hollywood filmmaking. It resonates because it contains something truly special: genuine emotion.

"People like to feel things," explains Brian Volk-Weiss, director of the series *The Holiday Movies That Made Us*. "It could be happiness, with laughter, or it could be sadness, with crying. It can be shock. It can be horror. But I think ninety-nine percent of movies do not make you feel something. You may be entertained, you may enjoy it, but you don't have an involuntary, visceral reaction to a moment or a song or an event or an action or a line of dialogue. Only one percent of movies make you feel something. That's what makes it connect. Every movie I love or that we've done shows about makes you feel something. This movie makes you feel a lot of things."

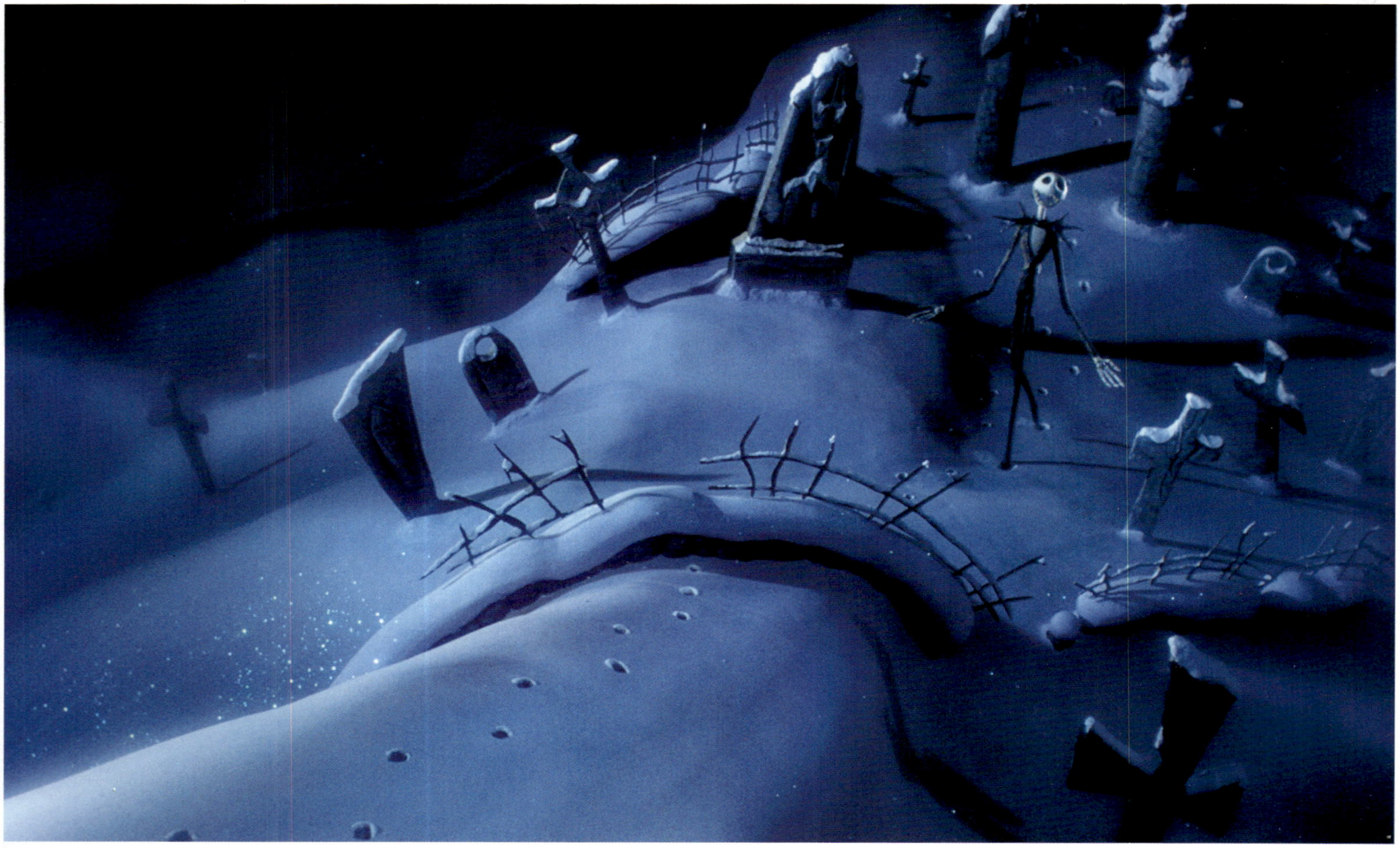

THE *NIGHTMARE* LIVES ON

Over the years, *Tim Burton's The Nightmare Before Christmas* has created its own community. Fans connect over a shared love of the stories,

SHOT BREAKDOWN **Updated 4/20/93**

Set Up 8/30/92 Light 3 Prep 2 Shoot 5 Date Seq. Sched to begin 12/18/92

Shot# 1400/11 Sketch # 9A - 9H

Song: Jack & Sally Duet

Location: Cemetery

Time of day: Night

Description
WS - Jack and Sally embrace and kiss on Spiral Hill. Zero enters into frame and flies across frame to other side of Spiral Hill. TILT UP with Zero as he flies in a circle and disappears into a starburst.

Characters Needed
Jack, Sally, Zero

Character Notes
Happy dog

Sculpted/Fabricated Props

Model Props

Rigs

Notes

Dialogue: None

Approved [x]

Camera
Tilt. Safeguard camera move data for easy duplication on stars, snow, Zero elements. Give Pete fully documented camera move data for later snow matching.

Opticals
Zero composite

Cel Animation
None

Lights
Practical moon if move permits.
Pumpkins in the BG should be prepared to light up

Dissolves/Fades
None

Stage Set# CEM*5
Spiral Hill

Redressed with snow and winter FX; icicles, fiber optic glints, etc. Crunchable snow for footprints only where Sally & Jack walk. Hard snow where animators need to work.

Frame Count: 387
Seconds: 16.13

**Dates & frames WILL CHANGE. Check the big board for accurate dates and check with Editorial for accurate frame counts.*

and exciting, whether it's a detail in the set design, the reaction of a background character, or the way a song strikes a chord at that particular moment in someone's life. Every fan has their own reasons for their affection, their own sense of attachment, like they own a small piece of it, albeit one shared with millions of others.

According to Henry Selick, "It's not really mine or Tim's or Danny's anymore. It's the world's movie, and I kind of like that."

Christmas tree created by Tim Burton.

OPPOSITE TOP: Sally making soup using some unsavory ingredients.

OPPOSITE BOTTOM: Jack Skellington serenading Sally during the film's final musical number.

THIS PAGE: Early sketches of Sally created by Tim Burton.

ACKNOWLEDGMENTS

In 1993, I saw my first film in a theater. It was wondrous and magical, yet absolutely terrifying for a child. It had a memorable score, creepy characters, and was essentially a story about a well-intentioned experiment gone wrong. If you're picturing a rambunctious tot, mouth agape at the Pumpkin King, bopping along to Danny Elfman tunes, you've got the wrong image.

The first movie I saw in theaters was *Jurassic Park* (1993)—the film that was expected to annihilate stop-motion and change the future of animation forever. However, the release of *Nightmare* just a few months later would prove that regardless of flashy, more convenient methods of filmmaking, stop-motion could dazzle moviegoers in its own unique way that a computer couldn't quite replicate.

Though I didn't see *Nightmare* until a few years after its release, I feel eternally grateful that this film was made because it truly shaped my life and career by keeping this stunning art form alive. So, my first acknowledgment is to all the stop-motion animators in the world, many of whom I got to know during the writing of this book. You are amazingly patient and unique people, and I will forever be impressed by what you're able to accomplish.

Next, I am grateful to my editor Sammy Holland for her guidance, feedback, and friendship while writing this book. I also want to thank Justin Bolger, for being the great connector and recognizing this amazing opportunity for me. Thank you to Tim Burton for coming up with such a brilliant idea and chatting with me about it over thirty years later; I'm so grateful I got to hear his thoughts and mutually marvel over the art of stop-motion.

I'd like to thank everyone who worked on the film who graciously dug through their mental archive just to keep the memory of this production alive: Owen Klatte for sharing both his wealth of knowledge and interesting stories to make this book unique, Mike Belzer for talking me through the layout of Skellington and clearly explaining how he animated the famous "doorknob scene," Angie Glocka for her excitement to share as much information as she possibly could recall and for her gracious enthusiasm to lend her help in any way possible, Buck Buckley for his support of this book (and me!) and for a thirty-minute interview that was at least fifteen minutes of laughs, Loyd Price for sharing amazing, never-before-published stories and getting them to me despite the rush of the holidays; and Joel Fletcher, Anthony Scott, and Tim Hittle for taking the time to thoughtfully answer so many of my questions (plus clarifying questions!).

I'd like to thank Kat Alioshin and Todd Lookinland for producing the amazing *We Know Jack* podcast—the most valuable resource to me while excavating tiny details of the film's production. Listening to their podcast was not only a treat but adding the personal element from each crew member made sections of this book really sing.

Finally, thank you to my parents, for their lifelong support of my writing, my brothers for going trick-or-treating with me over the years (probably for too long), my husband who is living proof that "some of the best people are oddballs and weirdos," and my son for deciding to be born in October . . . so we can forever throw Halloween-themed birthday parties.

—DANA JENNINGS JELTER

OPPOSITE: A young Dana Jennings Jelter dressec up with her grandmother.

PAGES 174–175: A sketch of Jack atop the Spiral Hil by Tim Burton.

IMAGE CREDITS

Page 2 Walt Disney Animation Studios
Page 5 Walt Disney Animation Research Library
Page 7 Henry Selick
Pages 8–9 Walt Disney Animation Research Library
Page 11 Dana Jennings Jelter
Pages 12–13 Walt Disney Animation Research Library
Page 14 Walt Disney Animation Studios
Page 16 (all) Walt Disney Animation Research Library
Page 17 (all) Walt Disney Animation Studios
Page 19 Walt Disney Animation Research Library
Page 20 World History Archive / Alamy Stock Photo
Page 21 Allstar Picture Library Ltd / Alamy Stock Photo
Page 22 Pictorial Press Ltd / Alamy Stock Photo
Page 22 (bottom left) Walt Disney Animation Research Library
Page 22 (bottom right) Walt Disney Animation Research Library
Page 23 Everett Collection, Inc. / Alamy Stock Photo
Page 24 Walt Disney Animation Research Library
Page 26 Walt Disney Archives
Page 27 (left) Tim Burton
Page 27 (right) Walt Disney Archives
Page 28 (bottom left) Tim Burton
Page 28 (bottom right) Tim Burton
Page 29 (top) Walt Disney Animation Studios
Page 29 (bottom) Tim Burton
Page 30 (top) Tim Burton
Page 30 (middle) Tim Burton
Page 30 (bottom) Tim Burton
Page 31 (all) Tim Burton
Page 32 (top) Tim Burton
Page 32 (bottom) Walt Disney Animation Studios
Page 33 (top all) Walt Disney Animation Studios
Page 33 (bottom) Walt Disney Animation Research Library
Page 34 Walt Disney Animation Studios
Page 36 Angie Glocka
Page 37 (top) Tim Burton
Page 37 (bottom) Owen Klatte
Page 38 Walt Disney Archives
Page 39 (top) Owen Klatte
Page 39 (bottom) Anthony Scott
Page 40 Walt Disney Animation Research Library
Page 41 (top) Walt Disney Archives
Page 41 (bottom) Walt Disney Animation Studios
Page 42 Walt Disney Archives
Page 43 (top) Walt Disney Animation Research Library
Page 43 (bottom left) Walt Disney Animation Research Library
Page 43 (bottom right) Walt Disney Animation Research Library
Page 44 (top) Owen Klatte
Page 44 (bottom) Owen Klatte
Page 45 (left) Owen Klatte
Page 45 (right) Walt Disney Archives
Page 46 Walt Disney Animation Studios
Page 48 Tim Burton
Page 49 Tim Burton
Page 50 Tim Burton
Page 51 (top) Walt Disney Animation Studios
Page 52 (bottom) Todd Lookinland
Page 52 Animation Research Library of Walt Disney Animation
Page 54 (all) Walt Disney Animation Research Library
Page 55 Walt Disney Animation Research Library
Page 56 Walt Disney Animation Research Library
Page 57 Tim Burton
Pages 58–59 (all) Walt Disney Animation Research Library
Page 60 Walt Disney Animation Research Library
Page 61 (all) Tim Burton
Page 62 Walt Disney Archives
Page 63 (top left) Tim Burton
Page 63 (top right) Walt Disney Archives
Page 63 (bottom left) Tim Burton
Page 63 (bottom right) Walt Disney Animation Studios
Page 64 (left) Tim Burton
Page 64 (top right) Walt Disney Archives
Page 64 (bottom right) Walt Disney Animation Studios
Page 65 (top) Walt Disney Animation Research Library
Page 65 (bottom) Walt Disney Animation Studios
Page 66 Tim Burton
Page 67 Tim Burton
Page 68 (top) Walt Disney Animation Research Library
Page 68 (bottom left) Walt Disney Animation Research Library
Page 69 (bottom right) Walt Disney Animation Research Library
Page 69 (top) Walt Disney Animation Research Library
Page 69 (middle) Walt Disney Animation Research Library
Page 69 (bottom) Walt Disney Animation Studios
Page 70 Walt Disney Animation Research Library
Page 71 Walt Disney Archives
Page 72 (top) Walt Disney Animation Research Library
Page 72 (bottom left) Walt Disney Animation Research Library
Page 72 (bottom right) Walt Disney Animation Research Library
Page 73 (top) Walt Disney Animation Research Library
Page 73 (bottom) Rich Heinrichs
Page 74 (left) Walt Disney Archives
Page 74 (right) Walt Disney Archives
Page 75 Walt Disney Archives
Page 76 (top) Walt Disney Archives
Page 76 (bottom) Walt Disney Archives
Page 77 Walt Disney Archives
Page 78 Walt Disney Archives
Page 79 (top) Walt Disney Animation Studios
Page 79 (bottom) Walt Disney Animation Studios
Page 80 Walt Disney Animation Research Library
Page 82 Tim Burton
Page 83 Walt Disney Animation Research Library
Page 84 Walt Disney Animation Research Library
Page 85 (top) Walt Disney Animation Research Library
Page 85 (middle) Walt Disney Animation Research Library
Page 85 (bottom) Walt Disney Animation Research Library
Page 86 (all) Walt Disney Animation Research Library
Page 87 (all) Walt Disney Animation Research Library
Page 88 Walt Disney Archives
Page 89 (top) Walt Disney Archives
Page 89 (bottom) Walt Disney Archives
Page 90 Walt Disney Archives
Page 91 (top) Todd Lookinland
Page 91 (bottom) Walt Disney Archives
Page 92 Walt Disney Animation Studios
Page 93 (all) Walt Disney Animation Studios
Page 94 Walt Disney Animation Research Library
Page 95 Walt Disney Animation Studios
Page 96 Walt Disney Animation Studios
Page 98 Walt Disney Animation Studios

Page 99 (top) Walt Disney Animation Studios
Page 99 (bottom) Walt Disney Animation Studios
Page 100 Walt Disney Animation Studios
Page 101 (top) Walt Disney Animation Studios
Page 101 (bottom) Walt Disney Animation Studios
Page 102 Walt Disney Archives
Page 103 (top) Masheter Movie Archive / Alamy Stock Photo
Page 103 (bottom) Walt Disney Archives
Page 104 Walt Disney Archives
Page 105 Walt Disney Archives
Page 106 Walt Disney Animation Studios
Page 107 (top) Walt Disney Animation Studios
Page 107 (bottom) Walt Disney Animation Studios
Page 108 (top) Walt Disney Animation Research Library
Page 108 (bottom) Tim Burton
Page 109 (left) Walt Disney Animation Research Library
Page 109 (right) Walt Disney Animation Research Library
Page 111 (top) Jennika Argent / Alamy Stock Photo
Page 111 (bottom) Walt Disney Animation Research Library
Page 113 Walt Disney Animation Studios
Page 114 Walt Disney Animation Research Library
Page 116 Walt Disney Animation Research Library
Page 117 Tim Burton
Page 118 Tim Burton
Page 119 Walt Disney Animation Research Library
Page 120 Walt Disney Archives
Page 120 (bottom left) Walt Disney Animation Research Library
Page 120 (bottom right) Walt Disney Animation Research Library
Page 122 (bottom left) Walt Disney Animation Research Library
Page 122 (bottom right) Walt Disney Animation Research Library
Page 123 Walt Disney Animation Research Library
Page 157 © Insight Editions. All rights reserved.
Page 125 (top) Disney Press
Page 125 (bottom) Disney Hyperion
Page 127 (top) Walt Disney Animation Studios
Page 127 (bottom) Walt Disney Animation Studios
Page 128 Walt Disney Archives
Page 129 Walt Disney Archives
Page 131 Walt Disney Animation Research Library
Page 132 Walt Disney Animation Research Library
Page 134 Walt Disney Animation Studios
Page 135 (top) Walt Disney Animation Studios
Page 135 (bottom) Walt Disney Animation Studios
Page 136 (top) Walt Disney Archives
Page 136 (bottom) Walt Disney Archives
Page 137 Walt Disney Archives
Page 138 (all) Walt Disney Animation Research Library
Page 139 (all) Walt Disney Animation Research Library
Page 140 Walt Disney Animation Studios
Page 141 (all) Walt Disney Animation Studios
Page 142 Walt Disney Animation Studios
Page 143 (top) Walt Disney Animation Studios
Page 143 (bottom) Walt Disney Animation Studios
Page 144 Walt Disney Animation Studios
Page 145 Walt Disney Animation Studios
Page 146 Katerina Sulova/CTK Photo/Alamy Live News
Page 149 Photo by: Melisa McGregor
Page 150 Walt Disney Animation Studios
Page 152 Walt Disney Animation Research Library
Page 153 Walt Disney Animation Research Library
Page 154 Walt Disney Archives
Page 155 (top) ©2025 The LEGO Group. All rights reserved.
Page 155 (bottom left) Walt Disney Archives
Page 155 (bottom right) © 2025: Funko, LLC.
Page 156 © 2025: Funko, LLC.
Page 157 © Insight Editions. All rights reserved.
Page 158 © Disney
Page 159 Walt Disney Archives
Page 160 Used with permission from Hasbro.
Page 161 © Disney
Page 162 Walt Disney Archives
Page 163 Walt Disney Archives
Page 164 Colourpop Cosmetics
Page 165 Walt Disney Archives
page 166 Tim Burton
Page 168 (top) Walt Disney Animation Studios
Page 168 (bottom) Walt Disney Animation Studios
Page 169 Tim Burton
Page 171 Dana Jennings Jelter
Pages 174–175 Tim Burton

INSERTS:
Page 64 (all) Owen Klatte
Page 79 (all) Tim Burton
Page 99 Walt Disney Animation Research Library
Page 119 Walt Disney Animation Research Library
Page 139 (all) Walt Disney Animation Research Library
Page 169 Walt Disney Animation Research Library
Interior Back Cover (all) Walt Disney Animation Research Library

PO Box 3088
San Rafael, CA 94912
www.insighteditions.com

Find us on Facebook: www.facebook.com/InsightEditions
Follow us on Instagram: @insighteditions

Trade ISBN: 979-8-88663-149-4
Collector's Edition ISBN: 979-8-88663-533-1

Publisher: Raoul Goff
SVP, Group Publisher: Vanessa Lopez
VP, Creative: Chrissy Kwasnik
VP, Manufacturing: Alix Nicholaeff
Art Director: Matt Girard
Senior Designer: Lola Villanueva
Associate Editor: Emma Merwin
Executive Managing Editor: Maria Spano
Senior Production Manager: Greg Steffen
Strategic Production Planner: Lina s Palma-Temena

Portions of this book were originally published as *Disney Tim Burton's The Nightmare Before Christmas: Beyond Halloween Town: The Story, the Characters, and the Legacy* in 2023.

Special thanks to Mike McAvennie, Jim Fanning, Mike Buckhoff, Nicole Carroll, Kevin M. Kern, Rebecca Cline, Mary Walsh, Fox Carney, Doug Engalla, Jackie Vasquez, the Staff of the Walt Disney Archives, and the Staff of the Walt Disney Animation Research Library.

Insight Editions, in association with Roots of Peace, will plant two trees for each tree used in the manufacturing of this book. Roots of Peace is an internationally renowned humanitarian organization dedicated to eradicating land mines worldwide and converting war-torn lands into productive farms and wildlife habitats. Roots of Peace will plant two million fruit and nut trees in Afghanistan and provide farmers there with the skills and support necessary for sustainable land use.

Manufactured in China by Insight Editions

10 9 8 7 6 5 4 3 2 1

HALLOWEEN
TOWN